Dedication

To Robert and Trang, Daniel and Gretchen, travelers all

CONTENTS

ILLUSTRATIONS

Introduction

ANOTHER ROAD: MYTH AND PAVEMENT IN THE AMERICAN IMAGINATION

American myths are manifest in pavement. Freedom, mobility, escape, and opportunity, or at least the dreams of, are only an entrance ramp away. Our roads, especially interstates, have enhanced our various national myths, such as individualism—not traveling by train, rail or wagon, in a group. It is me and my vehicle. One person, one auto, on the road, in control. America's pulse is not felt so much in its natural wonders, national parks and expansive landscapes, as it is in the routes to such sights. Though worthy, the destinations are remnants of a frontier history and romantic ideals of a rugged cultural character. Roads have supplanted our wildlands as the expression of culture and character. Restlessness "unlike any that any race before has known" is intrinsic to the national character. As James Agee noted, "we move for no better reason than the plain unvarnished hell of it."[1] In our cultural soul, the roads are the arteries and veins of an ephemeral identity. Even in this age of digital tyranny, asphalt reigns in our daily activities, our memories, our plans.

This book is an attempt to traverse a slightly different—but not foreign—route in considering our cultural penchant for motion and meandering. In contrast to much of what is written about roads there is no pretense of discovering America or myself. In my 70th year, I'd damn well better know who I am, and if I don't know where America is by now, there is no hope of ever doing so. The very idea of writing about roads is a rather pedestrian concept, given the flood of books, articles, movies and various videos, even songs, that tackle the idea, some quite artfully and imaginatively, others more ineptly. Who are Americans, or what is the kernel of the national spirit? No idea. No hope of approaching, let alone answering, such a riddle. Instead, this concerns some select values, or myths, and the role of highways in directing and supporting them. Thus, the trip becomes a curiosity, not a quest. Among other things, it is a nation rich in myth and pavement. That the road itself is the frontier is supported by the fact that no place in the lower 48 is more than 20 miles from some sort of highway.[2]

Though it is the auto that enthralls, the road anticipates it by a few centuries of trails and exploration. Autos just made the roads more utilitarian and democratic, available to more people. Roads exist at a critical juncture: The reality under our wheels, and the transition to our imaginations. They deliver us regularly from the overly familiar paths and into parts unknown, which might be a national park 2,000

---

1   James Agee, "The Great American Roadside," *Fortune*, July-September 1934, vol. 10, pp. 53-63, 172-174, 177.

2   Philip Caputo, *The Longest Road: Overland in Search of America, from Key West to the Arctic Ocean* (New York: Henry Holt, 2013), 52.

miles away or a yet-to-be-perused used bookstore the next town over. Roads are reliable routes to making a living, whether the office, the job, or robbing a liquor store. They are escape and assurance, paths to the past and conduits to tomorrow, freedom from and confinement in the commuter life. No one waxes eloquent about pavement, only the cars upon them. For some, getting wistful about the classic autos—for me, say, a '57 Chevy—would be pointless without the classic yellow and white lines on asphalt to expedite breaking the speed limit, making one a latter-day scofflaw.

We might think of pavement as an expression of civilization and civilized travel. However, roads are one definition of adventure in this paved nation. They have not displaced the national self-image of individualism and frontiersmen any more than modern firearms such as AK-47s have diluted the myth of the 19th-century pistol-toting cowboy. Now, that individualism and spirit of adventure simply have found a new expression. Adventure often is correlated to distance as much as place, i.e., it is more adventurous to drive cross-country on an interstate than to go cross-town on city streets daily for years on end, though the latter may be far riskier.

We have become pioneers on pavement, in reality and in our imaginations. Once upon a time, the frontier was a safety valve. Roads have assumed that function, even if done less dramatically on pavement than on wilderness paths and Conestoga-wagon trails. According to historian Frederick Jackson Turner writing in the late 19th century, the frontier shaped and eventually helped define the American character. That frontier is gone, and in that respect, according to another author, the nation has lived past the end of its myth.[3] But good myths die hard,

---

3   Greg Grandin, *The End of the Myth: From the Frontier to the Border Wall in the Mind of America* (New York: Metropolitan Books, 2019), 271.

and the frontier is a good myth. The idea of a frontier persists, in no small part, due to roads into remote areas and faraway places.

Roads are immediate, here and now, every day. Their existence is presumed, like frontiers once were. The frontier myth is so persistent that even as late as 1970, a U.S. Department of Agriculture publication touted the American wilderness and remaining "untamed lands" available to the American people.[4] Naturally, it was and is of no consequence to our restless souls and spinning wheels that something might be both "untamed" and easily accessible. Roads enhance that durable contradiction. Ingrained in our daily existence and movement, roads amplify what we extol in people—independence, individualism, the impulse to explore, the urge to just move.

It is a paradox as to whether a frontier can even exist without a road. How can it be a frontier if you don't know it's there, or if it has boundaries? The earliest roads in continental America were water ways, which were simultaneously routes for and barriers to travel. These "ways" went to other places, even frontiers' edges. Following such byways, roads came, dirt at first, asphalt eventually.

Given the expanse of America, we came to fancy ourselves a culture of frontiersmen. To some extent, we must be, given the pervasiveness of the frontier in our national mythologies, our media, and even in political utterances, i.e. "New Frontiers." We cling to frontier as defined in the 19th century via film, literature, fiction, etc. It works fairly well, persisting in spite of the fact that it no longer exists.

---

4   James Oliver Robinson, *American Myth, American Reality* (New York: Hill and Wang, 1980), 113.

1763 - The Boston Post Road

The Boston Post Road, In 1729, ran from north of the
Massachusetts Colony to Philadelphia. A letter from Boston
to Williamsburg, Virginia, took a month. The artwork is by
Carl Rakeman, who joined the Department of Agriculture in
1921, beginning several decades of paintings for the Federal
government. He retired from the Bureau of Public Roads
in 1952. With BPR, he painted exhibits for the Good Roads
meetings, state fairs, and expositions. His work included a series
of 109 paintings depicting historic American roads, trails, and
highways. They are available at various government websites,
not just the one noted here: https://highways.dot.gov/public-
roads/januaryfebruary-2002/legacy-art-new-exhibition

Pavement is a cultural skin, another route into the national
wildlands, the mythic foundation that embraces frontiers and promotes

progress. Roads take us somewhere new, a personally undiscovered frontier that may be under our feet, or under our car tires. And so roads amplify prevailing and traditional myths such as individualism and egalitarianism. This is how many lost souls still find meaning in near-inaccessible places, a road being essential in finding any oddball's Eden.

Mythic vitality

Myths are not lies, but reality writ large, reflecting values, enhancing and even defining them. Like roads and automobiles, myths are dynamic and changing. They evolve with culture and, in something of a contradiction, preserve it. Myths are a way to embrace contradictions, a way to resolve tensions arising from incongruity in values. Our myth of egalitarianism, for example, has persisted across more than two centuries in spite of discrimination and obvious gaps in wealth, political power, and opportunity.

John Steele Gordon, in an *American Heritage* article, deemed automobiles the "invention that changed the world." His case is solid. But in that issue of *American Heritage*, dedicated to the national love of autos and their historical impact, the road is taken for granted, merely assumed. However substantial the impact of cars—on culture, economy, values, etc.—they require pavement. The auto and the road are symbiotic. Autos in the 20th century were even more substantial in their impact than the railroads of the 19th century, he argues. Autos altered the landscape, economy, social morays, daily life, communities, and environment. As early as the 1920s, automobiles were the largest sector of the economy. That impact is seen, too, in other industries, including glass, oil and rubber. All of this presumes the road. Beyond cities at the end of the 19th century, paved roads were simply not needed. America's 200 miles of pavement in 1900 were up to 187,000 miles by 1910. As early as the 1920s, a system of highways, interstate no less, was in its genesis, though nothing like the interstate system that emerged in post-WWII America.[5]

Among American mythic symbols, roads may be unique because they are both the symbol that embodies values such as mobility, individualism, and rebellion—and are the mythic entities themselves. They are both the destination and the route to destiny. The road is the goal. Just as the concept of frontier is fluid and changing, so is idea of "road" changing. It may be a dirt path, a mountain pass or an interstate highway. It may be just an idea, not yet a physical thing. Such routes may be like the Lewis-and-Clark quest to find a waterway to the Pacific, trying to affirm the existence of something—a way—that did not yet exist. But in the early 19th century, it was not a question of whether such a thing even existed. It was a question of finding it. Similarly, the legendary Northwest Passage, which cost so many ships and lives, must have been there, even if it was not.[6] Turner asserted that the frontier had done nothing less than fashion "a formula for social regeneration."[7] Now, thanks especially to the interstate system, such regeneration is an annual event for many, into our frontier remnants. The road trip, the vacation, is a vital ritual.

The route to regeneration can be a Sunday drive, a summer vacation, or complete relocation to somewhere else, maybe the suburbs or the countryside. These regenerative routes are commonly away from an urban area. The idea that cities are places of sin is at least as old as the Book of Genesis, note Sodom and Gomorrah. The latter

---

5   John Steele Gordon, "Engine of Liberation," *American Heritage*, November 1996, 42-45, 52.

6   See Grandin, especially chapter 7, on the changing idea of frontier.

7   Robinson, 114.

memorialized to this day in language. Cities remain places of unseemly sights, such as garbage on sidewalks, rats in alleyways, smog in the air, horns blaring, and so on. It's a common image of urban life, with the sins of the countryside overlooked in favor of greenery and blissful solitude. The way to that latter's presumed serenity, whether for a summer sojourn, or for permanent residence, is the road.

Roads are a path to freedom, opportunity, riches, and so on. They put someone in control of his or her own destiny in a way that mass transit cannot. Much of writing and video about roads seems to reflect an activity that is done, as Agee said, simply for the hell of it. For example, the first transcontinental automobile trip, by Horatio Jackson in 1903, was "purely for pleasure and to satisfy an enthusiastic motorist that it could be accomplished," according to the Boston *Herald*.[8]

Cars reflect our culture in myriad fashion. One notable way is in contrast to European cars, of style and elegance, or Japanese cars, which seem to fixate on dependability. American autos are about power and speed, the faster the better.[9] By extension to roads, the only thing to envy about the Autobahn is the fact that no speed limit exists. Among other things, the pursuit of happiness is one of our inalienable rights. What better way to pursue it than to hit 70 or 80 on the interstate. Or better yet, as per advertising hype, one needs to venture into the wilds via a four-wheel drive vehicle, maybe it's a pickup truck, and strike out for muddy roads and rocky paths in high places. The road is available to all, in a way the frontier never was. In this respect, the road feeds our myths of frontier and egalitarianism.

---

8   Dayton Duncan and Ken Burns, *Horatio's Drive: America's First Road Trip* (New York: Alfred A. Knopf, 2003).

9   Gordon, 49.

Travel writers often have a common suspicion, if not outright hostility, to more modern modes of transport for the masses, especially interstates—vs. what? Stagecoaches, trains, horses, steamboats? Imagine a 19th- century writer bemoaning train travel to, say, the West Coast, in favor of horse or wagon. And so our 20th and 21st century writers often imagine they see people shaped by the land around them, homogenized and robbed of regional character by the interstate that courses through the area. There must be some truth in the homogenization assumption, but the assumption is flawed, the idea that something is lost in the flow of people, rather like saying the aorta gets blood going through all parts of the system, and, thus, it is not good.

The "road towns" that emerged, morphed and grew along highways in the 1920s drew the ire of a couple of writers in *Harper's Magazine* in 1931. MacKaye and Mumford were sharply critical of such road towns and advocated bypasses without the attendant vendors, gas stations, inns that so fouled the local ambiance. They wanted "a roadway located quite apart from the towns with a wayside free from the eyesores of town growth; in short, a townless highway." But in looking backward they also anticipated the idea of an interstate system. Their implicit argument was for preservation of the town of pre-auto days. There was a kind of selective blindness in their bemoaning the perils and traffic snarls that paved roads would bring to towns, apparently in contrast to the mud streets and horse manure of yesteryear.[10]

There is great irony in the fact that roads are such iconic symbols in American myth, especially individualism, because road building is necessarily a collective endeavor for the collective good. In fact,

---

10   Benton MacKaye and Lewis Mumford, "Townless Highways for the Motorist," *Harpers Magazine*, August 1931, 347-356.

there may be no better example of the triumph of the collective than roads and road building. Yet, these byways are icons in the lore of individualism and independence, whether as a way into a western or northern frontier, or as mere means to meander, accompanied by presumptuous insights into one's own, unique thoughts. Explorers and travelers are an important part of our national story. Peary, Byrd, Clark, Neil Armstrong. However, their deeds were accomplished because of a massive team effort. This is a contradiction in American myth—the individual vs. the collective. Roads embody individualism and freedom. They are the means of connection and disconnection, leaving and building communities, rebelling against them while creating them. The communal accomplishment enables the solitary traveler and aggrandizes the loner.

The road enhances the individual spirit, the chance to accomplish … something. Clearly, this wasn't the first way that people got across the country or traversed distances. Boats and canoes, stagecoaches, railroads—but these were usually in groups of people, often necessarily so. Highways elevate the individual, the same way the lone gunslinger in the Wild West was made iconic in literature and on screen. Similarly, it is a route to control and independence, in a way unlike, say, railroads, which confined one to a passenger car, the scheduled stops, the lay of the rails. Highways facilitate and accelerate the movement that is intrinsic to the national story. It began with migration to America of a people who were rootless once they had left the Old World. They may have left the Old World out of desperation, assuming that to which they ventured had to be better. The promise of somewhere else has endured in American history.

Even more than a promise, roads have become the physical manifestation of what is nothing less than a constitutional right in

America. And that, as declared in various court cases as far back as the 1820s, is the implicit right, constitutional, no less, to movement. The Supreme Court said it is implicit in not only several amendments, but as recently as 2022, in Dalen v. South Carolina, said it is a "common right … under his right to life, liberty and the pursuit of happiness…". So when one hits the road, it is an exercise not only in whimsy, but of a critical right, maybe no less so than speaking one's mind in the public square.

An Emerging Mania

The early 20th century saw the auto-building industry erupt and road-building boom. The Lincoln Highway was the first cross-country road and an important historic accomplishment, but just as significantly it was a testament to our impulse to move and to the emerging obsession with automobiles. The Lincoln Highway ran from New York to San Francisco, originally going through more than a dozen states. In the 1950s, it was largely replaced with Interstate 80.[11]

Interstate highways have had an outsize impact on our cultural myths. They have amplified our mobility and individualistic impulses, diminished our frontier, expanded opportunity, all while homogenizing the uniqueness of myriad subcultures. To this day, local advocates bemoan the invasion of regional culture, whose violation is exacerbated by interstates. Those same advocates wallow in the benefits of federal government and the economic benefits of roads. The embrace of local culture and regional identity at times collides with the very idea of an "American character," which one might reasonably presume would

---

11   Earl Swift, *The Big Roads: The Untold Story of the Engineers, Visionaries, and Trailblazers Who Created the American Superhighways* (New York: Mariner Books, 2011), ch. 2, focuses on the Lincoln Highway.

be enhanced by a vast web of easily accessed, interlocking highways. Such an approach also leaves unquestioned the assumption that a local culture, unsullied by a stream of outsiders, is something good. Perhaps that character is more apparent in the motion of its people than in the entrenchment of its groups.

Traveloguers often disdain interstates, just as aficionados of the cinema arts are quick to condemn television. Something for the masses. But these things that define modern life have opened up a bigger nation, one not confined by physical access, but only by ambition, imagination, and the price of gasoline. The world and the nation are made more accessible to more people. Bemoaning interstates, with their easy access to cheap food and motels, is testament to vanity. It is an implicit lament for how much better it was "back then," a paean to what's not visible from the newer highways. The essential fault is that just anybody can go there now.

Roads on our bookshelves, TVs, cinema

It is much easier to travel a road than to explain why. The sagas of lone hero/traveler in the Wild West may have their epitome in the pulp fiction literature of the 20th century, a genre produced by the likes of Zane Grey to great popular acclaim and critical disdain. Such restlessness doesn't need a road, but the road helps ingrain such a value across the culture by making motion easier and faster. One of America's greatest writers, if not the greatest, Mark Twain, made a career of being restless and, better yet, writing about it. This included several travel books, *The Innocents Abroad* and *Roughing It*. It was his greatest work, maybe the nation's greatest novel, *Huckleberry Finn*, that is the pinnacle of travel, as Huck and Jim drifted down a river to freedom for both.

Later, Jack Kerouac's *On The Road* offered, in perfect contrast to Twain's morality, a pointless travelogue that succeeded famously, even classically, in endowing that pointlessness with meaning. In other words, the road is inherently meaningful. Maybe the best roads are the ones that matter the least, in terms of vehicle volume. That is the bias of some writers, as with William Least Heat Moon's *Blue Highways*, or John Steinbeck's *Travels with Charley*. It is not just the roads per se, the ones we travel or want to travel, whether attending to work and family or checking grand ambitions off the bucket list. These less consequential roads are the ones not taken, with apologies to Robert Frost. But these routes often matter more to travelers of the imagination.

Agee found in roads a web of pavement, commerce and the national character, the latter being restlessness, driven by and fueling so much that is American. He found that by the 1930s auto cabin camps had opened up long-distance travel to common folk, who readily found inexpensive lodgings from coast to coast. Conversely, MacKaye and Mumford, writing a few years earlier, bemoaned the erosion of local culture, succumbing to cheap eateries and crowded streets.[12]

The breadth and depth of road themes in popular culture is immeasurable. A thick catalog of any popular media could only glimpse the expanse of the topic and would be outdated quickly. When Willie Nelson goes "On the Road" he offers an anthem to movement. The music may be the band's destination, but the road is artistic oxygen.

Roads appear inevitably to be liberating in cinema and TV. For example, a road trip is at the center of *Thelma and Louis*. Two women take control of their fates, escaping bad marriages, sleeping in a motor inn, violating the socials norms and committing adultery at that inn. In

---

12   See Agee and Gordon articles on this theme.

the end, they control their destinies by leaving the road and driving off a cliff. Abandoning the pavement is purest rebellion against American society.

Television police and crime shows could not exist without high-speed chases and mean streets. One early television series, *Route 66*, followed a few adventurers down the road, which itself is something of a "so what" to the various exploits the characters have along the way. But they needed the road to get there. That road, Route 66, is itself a national symbol.

Roads Don't End

The road is the myth because it embodies the people and culture even better than the destination. How often does the conversation about one's summer sojourn delve into the mode of transportation, perhaps the distance driven, the things along the way, rather than particulars of the destination? Getting behind the wheel and driving off into the sunset recalls the cowboy myth—the individualist, strong and resilient. Tell the establishment to go to hell—go 60 through the 30 mph town center, and then get out of town. The road is the way to something else, hopefully better, and maybe an improvement because it is simply somewhere else.

We are not quietly desperate, to steal from Thoreau, but noisily mobile. We can step outside our habitual boundaries—geographically, mentally, emotionally—and move, leaving the moment and the place, to choose a direction, somewhere. It's an elixir for lost individualism in a vanished frontier.[13]

---

13   Robinson, 116, quotes *Walden*.

We remain ambitious and ambivalent—loving the sweep of the landscape and living in insulated communities, whether rural or urban. There is the impulse to find Eden "out there," if only temporarily. Such travel should affirm that we are undeniably a "melting pot," not of gruel, but a lumpy stew of meats and vegetables, ladled out on the pavement and digested in our imaginations.

It is not coincidental that busts of Abraham Lincoln and Henry Joy, the principal promoter of building a cross-country highway, are next to one another in Wyoming. Two great liberators are acknowledged side-by-side on a very American road—the Lincoln Highway. Going across the continent at the time was a Herculean task, across much mud and sand, innumerable mechanical issues to contend with inevitable breakdowns, and lots of shovels. We have progressed. Now, one only needs four wheels and credit card.[14]

The accomplishment is simply to have done it.

---

14 Pete Davies, *American Road: The Story of an Epic Transcontinental Journey at the Dawn of the Motor Age* (New York: Henry Holt and Company, 2002), 230.

Chapter 1

ROADS AND MYTHS

O ur roadsides are littered with stories and myths. And like the myths of the American West, America's roads began in the East and culminated in the West. They amplify or at least make accessible any number of myths, including the frontier, individualism, the charm of the farm, progress and opportunity, egalitarianism, the rebel, among others. Highways maintain and accelerate, so to speak, the idea of independence, which began with migration to America of people who were rootless once they left the Old World. They settled here and started finding and building ways elsewhere.

When history and myth are at odds, the myth may well prevail, perhaps may even be enhanced, as with cowboys and the Wild West. That figure and his environs remain vital in the national imagination thanks in part to roads that take people where cowboys might have been, or to towns, such as Abilene, Tombstone, Deadwood, where we can drive to experience the myth's remnants.

Myths are more than tales or exaggerations. They can express deeply held values of a culture, perhaps told as stories or maybe something more abstract, something all would agree on. For example, that an individual matters is presumed, and one need not even mention it, and perhaps it is best expressed in the obverse—how repulsive such a system is that renders the person a tool of the greater social good or the state, i.e., Stalinism. A myth, as used here, is not a tall tale or a fictional story. Myths transcend time and place. We might disagree about its reality in fact—such as living in a society in which all are equal—but there is no argument about the morality of the basic tenet of equality.[15] If myths do not help explain and understand, they at least provide a way to believe explanations and thereby achieve some level of understanding. These are principles that guide our lives, probably daily. Myths are not religious doctrines, guided by ritual and prayer, because we need no reminders of myths' existence. We wear them like a skin, guarding and defining the inner person and culture.

Two national myths are especially conducive to roads. Those are the frontier and individualism. The first was intimately entwined with the country home and the family farm as a motivator, which diminished greatly in the industrial and post-industrial society. Individualism remained strong, if for nothing more than the annual vacation ritual of heading down the highway, getting away. Initially, railroads facilitated such gauzy demonstrations of the nomadic self. The hardships of earlier travel modes, i.e., wagon trains and waterways, dulled the fervor of wannabe pioneers. But in the modern world, automobiles and highways made the brief sojourn easy and common, democratizing it. One no longer needed, ala Theodore Roosevelt, the

---

15   Robinson, xv.

wealth to buy a ranch and the time to spend getting acclimated and learning to ride a horse. The frontier is part of the general idea that the vast expanse to the West was, until the late 19th century, always there, always available to people, and even defining the character of the people, whether they went there or not, at least in the eyes of more than a few historians.

In addition, roadbuilding and automobiles facilitated the decline of railroads. Roads eventually offered access to more areas than trains. In the 19th century, rail was the most viable form of cross-continental travel, and though it opened up the country in many respects, rail was nothing like the democratizing force of cars and roads. Initially, the latter were no threat to railroads, since there were so few roads, even as cars became more popular. That changed in the 1910s and 1920s as state and federal government got involved in road building. Railroads were point to point. Get out at the station, and find another way to your ultimate destination.

Eventually, the more expansive roads system, cheaper and more reliable autos, the burgeoning number of motels, and improved pavement made the family vacation via sedan more attractive. Travel in an economy rail car just could not compete in terms of comfort, convenience, and ultimately expense. In addition, the same economy and flexibility of autos was applied to trucks, making freight shipping on roads more viable.

The appeal of cars versus rail makes the disruption of rail seem inevitable when cast in terms of certain cultural values. First, individual freedom. More roads meant more freedom to go where one wanted, when one wanted, schedules and stations be damned. Economy meant not just availability to more people, but a more democratic form of travel, more travel for more people to more places. And, of course, given the appeal of motion—speed. No loitering at the station. If one wanted to go a long way, it was just a matter of finding pavement, affording a Model T, say, and having the hutzpah to do so.[16] These byways are icons in the lore of individualism and independence, whether as a way into a western or northern frontier, or as mere object of the meandering literati and their presumptuous insights about one's own thoughts.

Romanticizing the road is part of the national myth. More often, it is not the road that is the lure, but that which it amplifies and accelerates—such as individualism and freedom, and myriad other cultural signposts. Rebellion, for example, is nothing unique to American culture or peculiar to a generation, say the '60s. In the post-WWII decades, though, autos and highways proliferated as expressions of rebellion. A generation made heroic simply tooling down the highway in an absurdly painted bus—see Ken Kesey's "Merry Pranksters." The point? None was discernable, except giving the middle finger to the establishment.

On myth and roads

The frontier becomes accessible, if not literally via our wheels, then at least in our imaginations. It is possible for anyone to go there. One can witness this City on a Hill, the well-worn agrarian myth made real. Individualism is expressed daily, perhaps more loudly on an annual basis. Daily, the commute to work means using one's own auto, versus mass transit and crowds; or it may mean leaving for a distant place.

---

16   On the history of railroads and the impact of auto travel, see: Albro Martin, *Railroads Triumphant: the Growth, Rejection & Rebirth of a Vital American Force,* (New York: Oxford University Press, 1992), 126-127; Christian Wolmar, *The Great Railroad Revolution: The History of Trains in America* (New York: Public Affairs, 2012), 303-305.

The rebel is radical individualism, seen in such television classics as "Route 66" or in cinematic classics as *Easy Rider*. Though not notable as cinematography accomplishments, they simply are classic "go to hell" films in which youthful angst is made meaningful.

Even egalitarianism is radicalized, with roads leveling the landscape and making this country accessible to all. Our "melting pot" ideal is exaggerated as we converge on the same roads, even to common destinations, but just as often to the exclusion of other tribes in the culture. Levy found uncertainty about such commonality being a defining trait. As he traveled around the country, he saw vertigo manifest in numerous ways, including nostalgia for an indivisible republic that never existed, and a deep, patriotic devotion to a nation defined by regionalism. The fragility of such identity is a symptom of a certain disorder that cannot find its center in a multifaceted, multicultural nation.[17] This puts the myths of progress and opportunity at a crossroads by providing a cheap and easy means of moving to a better place, and perhaps making that place less desirable to outsiders. Previously wild or remote environs were degraded, the unknown became known. But we still like to think we've escaped something, maybe to a frontier.

Such elasticity of interpretation may challenge the cherished national myth of American exceptionalism. In the past, discovering this garden might have been a grueling, cross-continent journey, with much risk and privation. An extensive road system, however, minimized such tribulation, shrinking the trial to something more akin to inconvenience—flat tires, gasoline prices, mechanical breakdowns—

---

17   Bernard-Henri Levy, *American Vertigo: Traveling America in the Footsteps of Tocqueville* (New York: Random House, 2006).

than life threatening. These myths merge and diverge like entrance and exit ramps on these national highways.

Roads can bring myths to life, and have done so innumerable times in American history. A notable example is the Lewis and Clark expedition. The trek brought Jefferson's vision of a transcontinental way from an ethereal idea to reality. That is not to say they found the water passage to the Pacific, but they did traverse the continent, and that idea of the cross-country highway henceforth was firmly planted in Americans' imaginations. It was only a matter of finding the road. When they reached the Pacific Ocean they were actually resurrecting an old idea—the passage to India, the same one Columbus had been looking for before a continent got in the way. The existence of such a passage also involved the dreams of incredible fortunes to be had with loads of ivory, spices, peacock feathers, etc.[18] In one respect, the ultimate accomplishment of Lewis and Clark may have been to simply go overland much of the way. Arduous but possible. In addition, Jefferson's vision of American's filling the continent moved to possibility, thanks to these pathfinders.

Perhaps most critically, roads became entwined with one of the great founding myths of America, according to Levy. It would be a "land promised and refused, lines of escape, shimmering horizons, the wall of the Pacific, the American dream—the last chance, in this world, to have even a whiff of that rite-of-passage experience that for centuries was the discovery by each individual, of America."[19] Without the roads, imaginary at first, reality later, those horizons would never have been reachable, the escape impossible.

---

18   Henry Nash Smith, *Virgin Land: The American West as Symbol and Myth* (Cambridge, Mass.: Harvard University Press, 1950), 17, 19, 22.

19   Levy, 16.

The frontier: Fuel for driving to the dream

Geography and terrain constrained impulses to head west, but did nothing to dampen the national imagination, which for earlier generations was somewhat corralled by price and inconvenience. Autos lowered the physical and fiscal barriers. Horace Greeley's admonition to "go west" was no longer tethered to youth and gender, as he originally cast it, or to risk tolerance and affordability. In the 20th century, with mass-marketed autos, cheap fuel and new miles of roadways, "the West" became accessible to nearly all. Roads and autos were equated with freedom and individualism in the same way wilderness once was. "The wilderness … keeps its strength and presence in American belief through constant, paradigmatic excursions of individual Americans into the available natural wilderness. …"[20]

The idea of the Wild West and the national surge in road building correlated nicely, as automobiles and byways took people to places that in previous years were only alive in the imagination, dime novels or the penny press. It is a problematic contradiction. The road and auto opened up a frontier, but the frontier had disappeared a few decades earlier. Unlike earlier times, though, people could get there with the advent of cars and roads. Roads and people tamed wilderness and made it accessible, but didn't that mean the wilderness was now dead if it was penetrated by pavement? If one bridged civilization and wilderness, how can the latter exist? Contradictions, however, are part of the very thing that cultural myths solve. In this case, the road may have killed the physical frontier, but it did not slay an idea so ingrained in the public imagination.

---

20   Robinson, 114, 12.

The frenzy of auto production and road building in the early 20th century helped move the frontier from soil to imagination. It was no longer a remote place, a chapter in our past. Now, it was real for anyone with modest resources and a sense of adventure. Because of the roads, the frontier had moved from place, to imagination, to experience. The myth not only endured, it became even more deeply entrenched in the culture, especially in the thriving mass media of the press and radio, and especially in books and film. In 1902, *The Virginian* brought a nameless cowboy to Wyoming, where he battled and bested the bad guys, won a damsel's heart, and lived happily ever after. The best seller became a model for the Western genre and cowboy hero. A year later, *The Great Train Robbery* was not the first Western film, but it was extremely successful, and the action-packed story helped create an enduring genre of cinema.

The West was not just a geographic place. "It also was the West of mind, of the spirit, a concept that for generations had reassured Americans of a place to go, even though most of them would not choose to move."[21] But they did move, perhaps not permanently, if only via the family sedan. And if one lived where the ideal already had been ravaged, i.e,. California, then one moved eastward, but traveled the "the West."

---

21   Robert G. Athearn, *The Mythic West in Twentieth Century America*, (Lawrence, Kansas: The University Press of Kansas, 1986), 10.

1795 - The Philadelphia and Lancaster Turnpike Road

This is a depiction of the privately built Philadelphia and Lancaster Road, about 1795, which was the nation's first long-distance broken-stone and gravel surface. It made more accessible territory northwest of the Ohio River. By the mid-1800s, Conestoga wagon and stagecoach companies were in decline, with the increasing use of railroads and canals. Following a half-century of disuse, the road recovered with the invention of automobiles. (The art is by Carl Rakeman. https://highways.dot.gov/public-roads/januaryfebruary-2002/legacy-art-new-exhibition)

There is irony with the West and roads in that the roads, in demolishing the frontier, had enlarged the myth by making it available to more people. Novels, press, tv, cinema and roads, all of them opened up the West, so that even though the reality of frontier and heroic individualism was long vanished, the popularity of the myth grew. Just as wind and aridity eroded the soil, roads and accessibility should have eroded the myth of the frontier. Instead, the myth grew richer.

The road and the auto are drivers, so to speak, of radical individualism. Of course, the modern "frontier" is not the frontier of yesteryear. But in modern America, the road itself is something of a frontier, especially for expressing individualism, often in terms of going someplace one has never been, even though it was conquered long ago by society. Roads redefined frontier, downward, from someplace "out there" and undisturbed by civilization to a place down the road, where one has never been.

The West often is viewed as the greatest expression of American individualism, but it is not. As with roads—a more modern reservoir of individualism—government, especially federal, was central to development of the West. That tough do-it-my-way rancher or wanderer is legend. And it came later. In the 19th century, the government help was welcomed, in such forms as the Homestead Act (1862) and building railroads. Paved roads came later and were just as welcome as their government predecessors.[22]

Though a physical wilderness or frontier may be beyond our daily experience, it is easily conjured up from our imaginations. For example, the "new frontier" of American politics was a powerful message for John F. Kennedy in 1960. Much of the mythic culture was written in the East, but lived in the West. In this respect, roads only followed the myth. Two years may mark the closing of the frontier:

---

22   H.W. Brands, *Dreams of El Dorado: A History of the American West* (New York: Basic Books, 2019), xv-xvi, 303, 480.

1890, when the U.S. census found it vanished; and 1893, when Turner presented his thesis on the significance of the frontier. However, within a few decades, the frontier was resurrected. It was no longer a remote, desolate area, with the menace of wildlife, natural disasters, attacks by natives. It remained to be challenged and conquered. In 1903, Horatio Jackson went cross country by auto with much trial and tribulation, via auto in dirt, sand, mud, and a little pavement. Subsequently, the Lincoln Highway Association was formed with the purpose promoting a national route to traverse the country, as well as promoting the emerging auto industry.

The reality of geography and the idea of a frontier are critical to understanding the national impulse to build roads. The Wild West's genesis in the national imagination occurred from about 1845 to 1880.[23] Dime novels and the mass press had begun to flood the nation with tales of Western heroes and wild men. The mid-19th century press was instrumental in firing the public imagination with ideas about the romance of the West. The Wild West, that is. In the decades before and after the Civil War, a receptive audience grew and the publishing industry boomed. Tales of main-street shootouts and figures such as Wild Bill Hickok were examples of the gross exaggerations for eager markets. After the Civil War, the West was ideal for reinforcing and re-inspiring tales of individualism and exceptionalism in the still relatively young nation.[24] The press flourished. Sensationalism sold, and the West was easily molded to accommodate the market for the incredible. In addition, the West became standard fare for theaters and traveling

23 David Hamilton Murdoch, *The American West: The Invention of a Myth* (Las Vegas: University of Nevada Press, 2001), 31.

24 Paul Ashown and Edward Caudill, *Imagining Wild Bill: James Butler Hickok in War, Media and Memory* (Carbondale, Ill.: Southern Illinois University Press, 2020), 29-30.

shows, most notable being Buffalo Bill's Wild West Show, which even journeyed to Europe.

That the West may not have been so wild and violent as Buffalo's Bill's shows or Hickok's tales professed and was largely subsumed by tales of gunfights, lawlessness, and the menace of Indians. However, tales of wildness in wild places sell much better than images of civil folk creating a civil society in which families and businesses could thrive. Travel to exotic places required inspiration, contrived in the 19th century, and exaggerated in the 20th and 21st centuries by, among other things, more novels, movies, television, and an auto-tourism industry in need of places and means for mollifying a demand for the Wild West. Roads took them there. Even the early journeys westward may have been far more civilized affairs than reflected in later novels and television shows, as those wagon trains would write their own rules and constitutions before setting out on their geographic quests.[25]

By the time of autos and roads in first few decades of 20th century, the mythic West was several generations old and well entrenched in the public mind. Of necessity, the frontier remained in the West, where the frontier last existed. These large, open spaces needed conquest, i.e., Turner's thesis of the frontier shaping the American character. Roads and autos came along en masse only a few decades after he presented his thesis in 1893. As though to confirm his idea, myriad non-scholars— most of whom never would have looked at his thesis, let alone read anything of it—set out with the enhanced tools of mobility to conquer the frontier anew.

---

25   On the myth of the violent West, see Thomas J. DiLorenzo, "The Culture of Violence in the American West: Myth Versus Reality," *Independent Review*, Fall 2020, 15:2, 227-239; Roger McGrath, *Gunfighters, Highwaymen, and Vigilantes: Violence on the Frontier* (Berkeley: University of California Press, 1984). That wagon trains wrote constitutions is pointed out in DiLorenzo, 228.

The road and automobile rise and conquest of the national habits and psyches occurred relatively quickly in the early 20th century: Ford began mass production of the Model T in 1908; the Lincoln Highway Association was formed in 1913 to build a trans-continental road; Congress in 1916 passed the Federal Aid Act, making national government an enduring and central actor in road construction; Yellowstone National Park, notably, opened up to autos in 1915. There were other parks, more funding, auto-factory starts and advances in auto production and pavement technology.

As the frontier receded, Americans sped to embrace it. This also helped fuel a national commitment to wild places and access to them. It was a time that accentuated Turner by turning up the volume on his idea—America was unique, its frontier special, and a person now could see it for oneself. The West was an inviting destination for people looking for an escape, if only temporarily, from the confines of the city, and the road system—eventually interstates—offered the quick out.

Inventors of the West

Three figures in particular had contrived a West of individualism, freedom, chivalry, honesty, integrity. Theodore Roosevelt was the cowboy in the White House. Owen Wister had written the *The Virginian*. Frederic Remington was a popular-magazine illustrator who had become a national artist, conveying images of gun-toting heroes, mountain men and cowboys. The imaginary West and frontier to which Americans would stampede as the highway system made it ever more accessible came to full mythologic status around the turn of the century with these three individuals leading the charge. Admirably rugged heroes displaced the hard, often ugly, reality of life on the range. Like Roosevelt, Remington was an Easterner, and he illustrated Roosevelt's articles for *Century* magazine, enhancing Roosevelt's hero status from the Spanish-American War and the charge up San Juan Hill. Remington illustrated a frontier that people wanted to hear about— and visit. His idealized, romantic rendition of the fading frontier and its heroic inhabitants perfectly complemented Roosevelt and another Easterner, Owen Wister, who was similarly enthralled with the West. He, too, saw a fading frontier. Remington met Wister in 1893 at, appropriately, Yellowstone Park. Remington talked him into writing a series for *Harper's* magazine. It appeared in 1895. *The Virginian* went through 15 editions in 26 years, and eventually became a play, at least four movies, and a television series that lasted for nine seasons.

The West these individuals invented became the West that demanded highway access—something that came to be seen as the real America, its heart and soul, the place where the nation's most revered values thrived, and even a source of rejuvenation. Eventually, that meant building a way into the so-called frontier, reality be damned. The idea prevailed, and the roads got paved, as they morphed from dust to asphalt.[26] Turner said traits of frontiersmen were part of the allure of West and the national myth. It was a place where "men were men," and the roads west made that part of the nation a shot of Viagra for American men, with highways providing dosage and direction for use.[27]

By the 1930s, tourism was a major industry for the region, in no small part due to frontier-like places such as national parks or to events such as the daily shootouts in Deadwood, S.D., between a resurrected Wild Bill and a bad guy. Hollywood had defined the frontier for entertainment purposes as cowboys, cattle drives, saloons and

---

26   Murdoch, 70-77.

27   Athearn 228, 234

shootouts. It worked. Popular literature found the frontier a great seller, probably beginning with Wister, and becoming a genre all its own.

Sometime in the 19th century, as the geographic frontier faded, people began to appreciate the wilderness as intrinsically valuable, not just useful for resources but something that could build character, morality and individual strength. As the frontier disappeared in the late-19th early-20th centuries, we began to think about preserving it, and accessing it. These did not seem to be mutually exclusive goals at the time, in the early 20th century, when road building and park development flourished. The road builders were not just facilitating movement, but entrenching even deeper in the cultural mien the idea that one might see and experience the frontier. Roads became the preservative of that essential American character who was a frontiersman and individualist.

In the 20th century, wilderness remained quite vibrant as a source of discovery and regeneration. As the technology of auto-mobility took hold, a mythic wilderness replaced the real wilderness. Access via pavement did not just fuel the myth but did so rapidly. Perhaps the embrace became even more enthusiastic. As Robinson states, "If we are to be true Americans ... there must be a wilderness."[28]

Perhaps the real death knell of the geographic frontier was the intrusion of the federal government in 1934 with the Taylor Grazing Act, which closed unreserved federal land to entry, ended homesteading and cheap land sales. Extraction and agricultural industries, including timber, livestock and mining, could access the land via government contracts. Government programs aiding development in the West mushroomed in the 1930s, as the attendant myths of independence

---

28   Robinson, 124.

and self-reliance became more imaginary than real with the growth of federal programs for the region. Those ideals of individualism simply moved to the drivers' seats.[29] But it was the roads that made the sights and the expanse available to anyone with a few weeks to spare, a car, and an urge to have a not-too-perilous adventure.

Roads transformed the frontier and amplified individualism. When Congress, in 1916, approved the Federal Aid Road Act, the national government provided matching dollars to state governments for building and improving roads. Five years later, the Federal Highway Act gave matching funds to states for designating "primary" roads to become part of a national, interstate highway system. The explosion of road building correlated with the rapid increase in auto production, which went from two million units in 1920 to five-and-a-half million in 1929. The West's open spaces were ideal for promoting the national urge to hit the road. Cities and suburbs flourished, and tourism became a leading business in the region. Tourism existed before, especially with railroads, but that tended to make it a business better suited to the well-heeled, with favorite destinations being dude ranches and luxury resorts. However, cheap autos, notably the $290 (about $4,600 in 2024) Model T Ford, made such travel an affordable middle-class endeavor. The national parks were a special draw. Cars were allowed into Mt. Ranier National Park in 1926; Crater Lake in 1911; Glacier in 1912; Yosemite in 1913; Yellowstone in 1915. Millions swarmed over the roads and into the parks and national forests. The frontier really was gone, but its remnants were available to more people than ever. The adventure into the wilds of such places as Yellowstone was often only

---

29   Michael P. Malon and Richard W. Etulain, *The American West: A Twentieth-Century History* (Lincoln: University of Nebraska Press, 1989), 96-97; see ch. 3 on the government programs of the 1930s that aided the West and westerners.

a matter of having the chutzpah to risk the long drive, the motels, the diners, and even campgrounds.[30]

Though the frontier was gone, one could experience the Wild West fantasy, even better than watching saloon cowboys at the cinema or on television. Oddly, if not in perfect contradiction, roads defined the modern frontier. Turner's frontier was the "meeting point between savagery and civilization."[31] He saw the frontier as a place of regeneration, a place where free land and free people could experience wilderness. Such an apparent contradiction is allayed in modern society by an annual sojourn to a far-off place, properly deemed a vacation, a respite from the constraints of civilization via autos and pavement. That one's wilderness might have pavement at the gate is not worthy of deep contemplation by most people. A tamed frontier did not mean a non-existent frontier. Grandin believed Turner's "gate of escape"—the frontier –had been corporatized. Now, the gate of escape was a highway entrance ramp.[32]

Mythology of the West and the frontier

Roads, or their precursors, mere wilderness paths and trails, bridged civilization and frontier. Even a title of classic frontier literature, *The Pathfinder*, is about one who is getting the place ready for civilization. Just as popular media invented such characters as Wild Bill Hickok, so did they invent a place for such a character to reside—the Wild West. The West is not a myth in its own right. Instead, it is an amplifier of existing national myths. For example, the cowboy is unique to the West, but is actually individualism writ large. The original

---

30   Malone and Etulain, 40-44.

31   Quoted by Smith, 251.

32   Athearn, 147; Grandin, 271.

frontier was just west of the Appalachians, but the vast expanse west of the Mississippi made the frontier even bigger in the 19th century. The rebel spirit birthed the nation, fired a Civil War, and then lived on with Westward sojourns, where there was even more room and opportunity to shun the establishment.

Roads make possible our paradoxical embrace of the frontier, which is wild in our imaginations and paved in reality. Simultaneously, we idealize the early denizens of such wild places—such as Boone and Crockett—in fact and in fiction because they abandoned civilization. Even in frontier days, the fictional character such as Natty Bumpo, the deerslayer and Boone's fictional counterpart, was a heroic literary success. But our vision is a romantic one, in which the deadly aridity of some place becomes sunlight flashing off the gossamer strands of our imaginary wilderness. The barbarism and primitivism are contained in roadside museums, where we can reconcile reality and imagination, or at least make their co-existence in the national imagination possible.[33]

The impulse of motion is amplified in a national habit noted by others, such as James Agee. Writing in *Fortune* magazine in 1934. He found the American road not just an incredible 900,000 miles of pavement, but nothing less than a way of life, a community unto itself. The roadside was an industry "founded upon just one thing, the restlessness of the American people." He admitted that defining such a trait was an evasive thing, but he declared the nation's "restiveness unlike that any race before has known." This spirit necessitated places to eat, sleep, destinations to rationalize the movement, and so on. Such movement was not provoked out of necessity. "We are restive entirely for the sake of restiveness. … we move for no better reason than plain

---

33   Smith, 52, ch. 6.

unvarnished hell of it. ... So God made the American restive. ..."
Hence, roads, highways, paths, trails that not only created a country,
but defined it. Boone, for example, is always moving someplace else,
whether to flee civilization or to find wilderness. American heroic
myth often is linked to such characters who are in motion. Given our
national history and geography, that motion is naturally Westward. [34]

Thomas Jefferson sent a couple of guys to find a way to the
Pacific Ocean, as he wondered what the new nation had gotten in the
Louisiana Purchase. He did not have in mind to create national heroes
for simply traversing what was then called the American desert. In the
1770s, Daniel Boone's fame was founded, in part, on his wilderness
trail. In the 1830s, Davey Crockett died properly—in terms of leaving
a durable myth—after having wandered around so much of the nation's
woodlands. The decades prior to the Civil War saw a group become
the stuff of legend as they traipsed the Western mountains west.
Those mountain men included the likes of Jim Bridger and Jedediah
Smith. Charles Fremont, the "Pathfinder," led three expeditions West,
and made his public name in doing so. His reports on the first two
expeditions were best sellers of the day, reprinted seven times by 1856.
It says more about the national mind than the man. Fremont made Kit
Carson famous by employing him as a guide, a good one at that.[35]

In the 1930s, the growth of roads and tourism helped enlarge
the frontier myth even as the place became more peopled. Athearn said
that "disciples of the western mystique were engaged in a stubborn
retreat" in the early 20th century, as modernization intruded. Paved
roads served both sides of the conflict. Part of the frontier disappeared

---

34   Agee 53-54; Smith, 53; Boone blazed the initial "Wilderness Trail."

35   Murdoch, 7, 32.

before travelers, as roads helped myths of individualism and family farms by making the presumptive Eden available to more people. Their ideals were given to experiences in an actual place. Paradoxically, the frontier myth needed public and political support in order to be sustained and protected. These routes to the wilderness created a dilemma. All that space fed a sense of American uniqueness and optimism. However, the roads to actually experience that special part of the country—one that may actually define, or at least amplify, the national character—means the frontier eventually would be conquered. As Wallace Stegner points out, the West is important because "we simply need that wild country available to us, even if we never do more than drive to its edge and look in." That is precisely what our modernized system does. It is preserved, not in reality, but in the imagination.[36]

While fiction, movies and television continue to be the devices that maintain the mythic West, it was the road that carried people to experience the frontier, to sample it, attest to its reality. This affirmed one's own virility, independence, adventurousness, all of which are components of the national ideals of independence and opportunity.

Individualism

Individualism thrived in Turner's frontier, but inevitably had to find an alternative expression with the end of the frontier. Local, state and federal governments helped elevate individualism via road building. As early as the New Deal, the travel ethos became manifest in the collective, as that grandly ambitious government program built roads and excited the travel ethos. The New Deal "put forth a new, common

---

36   Athearn, 74; quote is from Athearn, 221-222.

sense ethic that freedom in a complex industrial society required government intervention. ..." In that same vein, modern roads are a social enterprise with a façade of individualism. The *New Republic*, in a 1912 article, said extreme individualism was a vice. Up to that time, and in the Turner thesis, individualism was a virtue.[37]

Traditionally, an important component of American individualism is isolation, which began with the geographic nation itself being isolated from the old Europe.[38] Such a sense of being apart may have contributed to the romanticization of isolation in popular America, i.e., the lone cowboy of the American West, the mountain man, or the singular individual of so much fiction—even dogs, according to Jack London in *The Call of the Wild*. The auto and the road were both made by corporate effort and communal taxes and became a central expression of individualism in the 20th century. Such ideals collide with reality, as with the cowboy, who in reality was an employee, a rather lowly one at that. So it goes with the independent loner vs. the corporate man on a two-week vacation. In the latter case, the individualism is redefined, not so much loner as it is someone who is different, facilitated in many cases by the road.

The West was a great symbol of opportunity, but it was not alone in representing the dream. That beacon of opportunity could shine in cities as well. However, the West—and the roads there—were more romantic, more susceptible to fiction, television and cinema. The East dominated in the mediated vision of America, and so pushed a marketable West, which came to look more like the East as time passed.

---

37   Grandin, 176-179, 168-170.

38   Robinson, 76-77.

For Westerners, economics meant more reliability on Eastern money and Washington, D.C., generosity.[39]

The ideals of independence and individualism began with the founding document, "The Declaration of Independence" and "all men are created equal." Pavement has been a great way to move mythic power from the ethereal into the personal. To steal more words from Jefferson, independence is good and needs no justification or limits because the truth is "self evident."

The ironic individualism symbolized by the lone traveler on the American road is a healthy one. The single person is completely dependent on a corporate, mass-produced machine only able to move on government-funded pavement. It is a healthy contradiction because individualism, which could not exist absolutely, does thrive within reason. Contrast that to people who insist on absolute freedoms, such as speech or gun ownership, and are imprisoned by attitude, ideas collapsing in on themselves by killing the social order that birthed the right. A radical strain of individualism and mobility has been the source of much folklore. As roads have degraded nature, they have made it accessible, virtuous, and pretty.[40]

The myth of individualism is influenced heavily by various technologies, including automobiles, just as another historical aspect of that myth was that everyone in the past owned a horse. They had not. Horses were expensive. In some ways, the wide ownership of autos and the abundance of roads fired visions of the past in which everyone was mobile, ready to move on. As horses went from reality to radio, television and cinema, they became more pervasive in the national

---

39   Brands, 480.

40   Robinson, 234-235, 278, 351-35, on myth of change.

imagination. Similarly, the individual in the car, on the road, was in control—no one dictating route and destination. Rather like the lone cowboy riding into town from who knows where, and riding off into the sunset to the same place. The point was individualism and freedom. The machine and the road had created not only modern America, but re-created past America.[41]

Exceptionalism and egalitarianism

A Lone Ranger or solitary cowboy may be a window, too, on why mass transit has limped along in this age of desperate need for such a thing. The road amplified an exceptionalist impulse in which one could experience a phenomenal geography—the American expanse, whether urban, rural, or nearly untrodden—in a way uniquely one's own. Myriad roads make it easy to abandon a prescribed route and schedule, even a prescribed purpose. This might be a weekend jaunt or a months-long foray.

The road per se is indiscriminate. Its users are not, as the experiences of women and Blacks has shown. Roads are democratic, leveling the landscape and making this country accessible to all. Autos were important in liberating women, providing not only mobility but equality in that mobility. As women took to the road on their own terms, they moved forward the idea that women could do what men did. Women had been driving for several decades before approval of the 19th Amendment in 1920.[42]

The leveling, or egalitarian, impact of roads and travel was emerging in the 20th century and was exemplified with publication of *The Negro Motorist Green Book*. Its first edition in 1937 advocated not

---

41   Robinson, 190-191.

42   Gordon, 59-60.

just minority rights but free movement, specifically by auto and roads. By the 1950s and 1960s, it was advocating direct action for civil rights, and saw that travel was an important way to defeat prejudice. Motion was a democratizing force.

The publication changed names numerous times during its lifetime. Its original publisher, Victor Green, died in 1960 at the age of 67 and so did not see the legal end of racial discrimination. He declared that someday a separate travel guide for Black Americans would not be needed, and Blacks could stay at any hotel or motel. In its first edition, *The Green Book* pointed out that white travelers had no difficulty in finding accommodations. It was different for Black motorists. *The Green Book* was one of a number of publications, and perhaps the most famous, that emerged in the 1930s, compiling lists of information for Black motorists. These guides not only facilitated travel for Black Americans, but also promoted equality by promoting a Black middle class, one that purchased autos and spent money motoring around the country. *The Green Book* helped travelers not only get across the country, but helped them maintain a sense of dignity and propriety.[43]

The Green Book and similar publications saw themselves as part of the fight against segregation. The first guide focused on New York City, and was filled with ads for eateries and car-care businesses. It warned Black travelers to avoid mechanical problems on the road, leaving them in potentially dangerous situations. It began as a 16-page pamphlet and ended its 30-year run as a paperback of more than 128 pages. With the growing civil rights movement of the 1950s and 1960s, *The Green Book* was part of the expanding freedom to move. By 1951, it had begun listing lodging in Canada and Mexico, even Costa Rica, Bermuda, the

---

43   Gretchen Sorin, *Driving While Black: African American Travel and the Road to Civil Rights* (New York: Liveright Publishing, 2020), 252-254, 164-167.

Virgin Islands and other international destinations. Members of *The Green Book* staff saw themselves as part of a greater movement that included the Urban League, the NAACP, and the Congress of Racial Equality. The road was a route to freedom.[44]

The road became a modern Declaration of Independence in May 1961 when the newly created Freedom Riders assembled in Washington, D.C., as part of the larger civil rights movement of the era. In particular, they were aiming at interstate travel on buses in the South. Perhaps at no other time in American history has freedom been more strongly associated with travel and motion—and consequentially—than in that summer.

The movement was preceded by several decades of activism, especially in the South, to ride public transportation and interstate buses. Many activists felt that transportation was the crux of second-class citizenship. In the spring of 1961, activists from the Congress for Racial Equality launched a campaign to challenge segregation on interstate buses. They had behind them several U.S. Supreme Court decisions, in 1946 and 1960, that ruled segregated buses were unconstitutional.[45]

The first riders left Washington, D.C., May 4, 1961, with New Orleans as the destination. They would end up riding across five deep South states, reaching their destination via a flight from Birmingham, Alabama. The Freedom Riders reached New Orleans during the night of May 15-16, but for the riders themselves it was more than a journey from Washington to New Orleans. The highly publicized ride to New Orleans met with numerous incidents of violence, arrests and beatings,

---

44   Sorin, 181, 194-195, 209, 204, 214.

45   Raymond Arsenault, *Freedom Riders: 1961 and the Struggle for Racial Justice* (New York: Oxford University Press, 2006).

but in a few places found a peaceful reception, such as getting served at lunch counters. The whole endeavor equated the very American ideals of freedom and motion. Freedom Rider and Rev. Bergman Cox told a reporter the rides "proved what we set out to prove—that American citizens cannot travel freely in the United States."[46]

The Freedom Ride Museum opened in Montgomery, Alabama, in 2011. President Barak Obama named the city's bus station the "Freedom Riders National Monument." Like a lesser known but equally important endeavor for justice, *The Green Book,* the Freedom Riders put to the fore of equality the idea that it is a nation in which motion and equality are a right.

In days well before roads, the idea that one could move was equated with opportunity. Whether the movement was from one city to another, from city to country, from country to city, it was a freedom to seek opportunity. One historian of national myths stated, "Movement fuels the belief in unlimited opportunity and ultimate success." For some, movement was hope, such as Steinbeck's Joad family in *The Grapes of Wrath.* They were exercising their freedom to move in the context of the motion-is-progress myth. It is done on the road.[47]

There is an "implied right" of mobility and freedom to roam. This complemented existing ideals of America as land of mobility, whether it is the freedom to move to frontier or up the economic ladder, or to the suburbs. The landscape sweeps over insulated people and communities. The nation becomes an Eden of opportunity if one is willing to travel to it, to risk failure in pursuit of success, whether economically or spiritually.[48]

---

46   Arsenault, 177.

47   Robinson, 241-247.

48   Swift, 271; Levy, 238-242.

A radical individualism romanticizes rebellion and rebels, i.e., the "Lost Cause," which saw the Civil War not as a fight to destroy the union and preserve slavery but as an endeavor to preserve an idealized lifestyle. The road can exaggerate the virtue of rebellion, even endowing pointless rebellion, without goal or destination, with meaning and purpose. The act itself—the auto or motorcycle on the highway—becomes mystically significant. Just cutting loose and driving down the road, across America, is an expression, a pronouncement, of something—whatever that is. The longer the journey, the more profound the something becomes. Exemplary in this respect are movies such as *Easy Rider* (1969) in which two free spirits, very anti-establishment, embark on a drug-financed trip. The only way to get rid of them at end of movie was to kill them with two redneck anti-heroes. This also embraces the myth of individualism. Similarly, Hunter Thompson, in *Hells Angels* (1967), made motorcycle thugs into heroes.

Travel has not been so much to learn about others as it is to learn about ourselves. It was a way to bring home national virtues, of "freedom, independence, isolation, equality, democracy. ..." No one lives in the wilderness in modern America, and can only experience it in their imaginations, perhaps imagine themselves as experiencing it, if only fleetingly, in a brief sojourn down the road. Americans used roads as a path to wilderness, whether it was real or imagined, and it was the latter so often in reality, though its place in the imagination was important. This idea of wilderness as a place of finding oneself appealed to American myth. According to Robinson, it was Thoreau who "made nature and the wilderness... . the central operators in the creation of Americans. After Thoreau, more and more Americans came to believe that it was the wilderness which made them American." Roads got us there, and still do.[49]

A route to Eden?

The garden myth goes hand-in-hand with the national frontier myth. Moving "out" to one's own garden spot often meant moving away from the city, or further westward, where more land was available. Still, cities were and are opportunity. The farm, the countryside, is nirvana, ala the Eden myth. With autos and highways, both are possible. Suburbs are the compromise, but roads and cars enabled the embrace of the dual myths of opportunity and Eden.[50]

There is an impulse to find Eden, one's own place, piece of land, where long ago wheels vanquished frontier. The rush to road building the 1920s correlated with the farming depression. Many farms failed and farming populations declined, shrinking from about 31.4 million in 1920, to about 30.2 million in 1940, and only 23 million in 1950. Cities grew. Farms declined. The frontier idea persisted.[51]

A frontier is not uniquely American, nor is it, obviously, anything new to humanity. However, the road makes the physical remnant of the idea more accessible and helps adapt it to American circumstances. The nation itself was an Eden to those in the past who might be leaving starvation, poverty, tyranny, for a chance to be free. In the past, finding one's garden might be grueling, difficult cross-continent journey, with much risk and privation. The road, however, minimized such tribulation.

---

49   Robinson, 117.

50   Robinson, 225-239, 234, 247.

51   Malone and Etulain, 19.

A pervasive and historical national myth—the frontier—found the road a perfect complement and preservative.

An Old Friend

Something of an icon along rural highways and even state routes, the rusted roadside remains of an auto are part of the American landscape. It is testament perhaps to an indifference to yesterday's accomplishment and grandeur, and the ever forward-looking move on down the road. (Painting by Jim Stovall)

Chapter 2

OUR HISTORY IS A ROAD

Trails, paths, passes and ways were a prelude to our mania for cars and pavement. Eventually, creating a nation meant finding the common threads, which weren't always there. But the ideas were there, and it meant connecting physically its various parts. It has been stitched with asphalt. Cars needed roads, and roads needed cars. America's disparate parts, geographically and culturally, discovered one another with asphalt.

All that land, even before there was a United States of America, provoked people to get out there. That started, depending on how one defines a "road," before the 1740s, when post roads connected cities. Those roads were often little more than paths. The Boston Post Road connected Boston to Springfield and came about when King Charles II told governors of the New England colonies he'd like better communication among the colonies, which was conducted primarily by ships at the time. Creating the inland connections was reasonable given that what became the United States was originally a group of coastal colonies. It was 1750 before the "King's Highway" existed for wagon and stagecoach travel from Boston to Charleston, S.C. The King got his wish, but with the Revolutionary War, such a name could not be suffered, so it became the "Boston Post Road."[52]

These early roads did what they were supposed to do: connect the colonies. That may have been an unfortunate side effect, from the King's perspective, as such roads later facilitated the conduct of war against the crown. Early roads also expedited travel to the frontier, and so the national flame was lit, over which our motion impulse has simmered ever since. There was a lot of room, a lot of land out there. The roads were the geographic safety valve's on-switch. Cities were dirty, many new immigrants impoverished. A lot of people went west. It was opportunity for some, escape for others.

The pursuit of happiness is among our inalienable rights, along with life and liberty. In contemporary America, a great way to pursue that right is to hit 70 or 80 on the interstate. The "New World" looked to the future and change, anticipating something better ahead—and the ideal fit well with roads that were to come. When our ancestors came to the New World, whether in colonial days or subsequent centuries, they anticipated something better ahead. That mien fit well with roads and autos that came later, as well as the national agnosticism about the past, unless it is ideologically useful. With the help of a dash-mounted GPS and an I-phone camera, eyes and minds tend to be on destination, not

---

52   William Dollarhide, *Map Guide to American Migration Routes, 1735-1815* (Bountiful, Utah: Heritage Quest, 2000), 1-2.

the miles left behind. Those miles are the past, faintly visible, if at all, in the rear-view mirror.

Before roads and autos, Americans were spread over a large continent. Socially, America already was a contrast to Europe, which was rich in people and poor in land. America was the obverse. Socializing was a local affair. Going to town may have been a day-long endeavor in the horse-and-buggy days. Autos and roads changed that and connected more people, who were no longer confined to the extremely local area. Such things as romance went from a neighborly indulgence to a regional tryst, and distance could also mean some liberty from family and inevitable supervision.[53] That aspect of automobiling may have reached its pinnacle in the 1950s and '60s with the drive-in movies and sedans' large back seats.

Some towns along the earliest roads were little more than a tavern, an inn, and a stable.[54] As early as 1867, the *Atlantic Monthly* took notice of the distinct nature of American travel, vs. European. The American proclivity to move was in sharp contrast to the European habit, even pride, in staying put. The article begins: "No people travel more than the Americans, whether inside of their own country or outside of it. Locomotion belongs naturally to the restless, shifting phases of the national temperament. Migration at home has become so general a habit, that cases of strong local attachment are almost exceptional...." Even in modern American culture, the restive impulse often is received with some admiration—i.e., having resided afar, or gone on lengthy travels—as opposed to the person who never leaves town. In part, the differences were reflected even in government, with

---

53   Gordon, 42-63. 56, 59-60.

54   Eric Jaffe, *The King's Best Highway: The Lost History of the Boston Post Road, the Route that Made America* (New York: Scribner, 2010), 12.

European governments wanting to regulate movement, whereas the
U.S. government is "anxious to have the individual entirely free...."
There was cost, in that "the refined, the brutal, the clean and the filthy,
the invalid and the swearing, tobacco-squirting rowdy, are packed
together...." In the context of railroads, European travel offered better
food, smaller crowds and more polite fellow travelers. Safety and
comfort were sacrificed to speed and reliability of travel.

Rail travel could be hazardous. "The shock of a catastrophe
makes but a temporary ripple on the swift, seething, impetuous
current of life...." It is a lament that seems still to apply, considering
the number of auto accidents and fatalities that are accepted as part of
daily life in America. The writer, in effect, was acknowledging values
of independence, individualism, and even a rebel spirit associated with
travel: "Our Anglo-Saxon race ...possesses less grace and courtesy than
any other of the civilized families of man. To the untaught American
mind courtesy implies a certain degree of servility..." Travel in America,
the writer concluded, is a "necessary annoyance."[55]

The first paved road was built only a few years after the creation
of the republic, and that was the Philadelphia-Lancaster turnpike,
which opened in 1794. It was stone and gravel, a toll road, privately
owned, profitable in the rich agricultural area, and it paid dividends
of up to 15 percent. Such private toll roads were common by the mid-
1820s, when agriculture still dominated with much livestock moving
over the roads, but there were ample numbers of people moving via
stagecoach and horse. It was a quick, heartening beginning to anyone

---

55 *Atlantic Monthly*, April 1867, "Travel in the United States," 478-484.

moving out to the frontier, starting on a road that was excellent by the day's standards.[56]

Roads became a federal concern when, in 1803, Congress designated five percent of sales of public lands to Ohio, a new state, for building roads. By 1806, the federal government began to plan an interstate road. The first section of the National Road was finished in 1818, connecting Baltimore to Wheeling, then in Virginia, and, after the Civil War, West Virginia. In 1838, the road was completed, running all the way to St. Louis. Now, it is roughly the route of Interstates 40 and 70.[57] In this respect, our modern interstate highway system is an old idea on a modern surface.

The first documented attempt to traverse the continent came about shortly after the Louisiana Purchase. The journals of Meriweather Lewis and William Clark became, in essence, our first national travelogue, replete with discovery, adventure, travails into unknown places among uncivilized people. The explorers' primary job was to find a way across the continent and to map the newly acquired Louisiana Purchase. Leaving from St. Louis, Missouri, in May 1803, their expedition took a little more than three years to get to Pacific Ocean and back. Instead of finding the "Northwest Passage," the presumed waterway that would take them to the Pacific, they found it wasn't there. This was the first—and maybe greatest—American epic. It is about finding a way, though certainly not a road, per se.

---

56   Geoffrey Hindley, *A History of Roads* (Secaucus, NJ: The Citadel Press, 1972), 86.

57   Dollarhide, 25-26.

Regeneration and motion

Woodrow Wilson wrote in 1895 that an alternative to a bleak vision of Civil War and saving the Union was to commit to moving outward. It was a way to "renew our youth and secure our age against decay." How American, asserting that the power of regeneration was to be found in motion. It was about the same time that Frederick Jackson Turner was finding the nation's frontier to be a dynamic source of character. Jefferson's and Turner's remarks reveal the critical role of motion in the national psyche. The Turner thesis is no longer fashionable, but the idea of an American frontier remains vibrant.[58]

Wilson's idea fits well with the notion that people might move, might go somewhere, might travel far. It is noteworthy that he did not attach any special purpose or goal to the motion, only that it was possible. It is a critical component of American self-identity and freedom. In the 19th century, there obviously was no collapse of industry and labor as the free land became available in the West. The freedom to move provided some modicum of relief for laborers. In the eyes of some thinkers, motion could cure a lot, such as the class divisions North and South—labor vs. capital, slave vs. landowner. With more decades passing and the ever-present possibility of escape, it is easy to see how driving down a highway evolved into a constitutional right.[59]

As early as 1850, one member of the House of Representatives, Caleb Cushing of Massachusetts, found the ability to move critical to

58   Grandin, 112. Grandin is basically a history of the idea of "frontier" from colonial days to the Donald Trump presidency. Chapter 7 is a good overview of the Turner thesis; Larry McMurtry, "Sacagewea's Nickname: Essays on the American West," *New York Review of Books*, 2001, 7.

59   Grandin, 77, 79, 82.

the very future of the nation, a "safety valve for all the pent-up passions or explosive or subversive tendencies of an advanced society." He called that national trait "expansibility." It was central to avoiding chaos and disruption.[60] Thus, even before the Civil War, freedom meant freedom from restraints, freedom to move, usually West.[61] Even in modern America, freedom is not an abstraction, but is physically manifest in, among other things, the freedom to hit the road. Movement, like breathing, is simply assumed to be part of one's life and citizenship.

The end of the 19th century saw the end of the national frontier, as defined by a line between civilized and wild, or settled and unsettled. By then, "the word 'frontier' had come to mean not a line but a way of life, synonymous with freedom."[62] It is used now with roads to so-called wild places, faux frontiers. McMurtry identifies three Wests: geographic, historical, psychological.[63] Roads have done much to eliminate the first, preserve the second, and invigorate the third. Getting "out" is very much a part of the social fabric, whether it means a sojourn to a wild place or simply a Sunday drive. It is as much a right as free expression and gun ownership.

As one of a litany of rights enjoyed by the nation's citizenry, it may be even more powerful than, say, expression or self-incrimination because motion is in the cultural fabric, not the social contract, i.e., the U.S. Constitution. A nation founded "on right of freedom, a right not just exercised **by** but originating **in** movement. ..." In fact, Jefferson, founding father and pre-eminent voice concerning Constitutional

---

60   Grandin, 82.

61   Grandin, 96.

62   Grandin, 48.

63   Larry McMurtry, *Roads: Driving America's Great Highways* (New York: Simon and Schuster, 2000), 9.

rights, espoused mobility as an essential right of people. The experiences of so many recent immigrants to the New World could be seen in his idea that people had a right to leave home and establish new places to live. One was not only exercising his rights in leaving home but taking part in a historic source of rights. It was deemed liberty. If liberty was threatened, then the solution was to move, to re-establish oneself. The dictates of the king did not follow.[64]

Ways to somewhere—and subsequently roads—have always been a part of our restless ancestors' imaginations, but the roads have not always been the domain of the automobile. When the League of American Wheelmen at the end of the 19th century launched *Good Roads* magazine, bicyclists were the target audience, and the purpose was better roads for cyclists. At the time, the cyclist was competing with horses, buggies, and carts. There were no traffic flow regulations, obviously. Riding a bike was challenging. If there was pavement, it probably was granite block or cobblestone, maybe even bricks. If that was not enough of a challenge, there was all that horse traffic—manure that splattered cyclists and strollers, endowing the area with equine aromatics. *Good Roads'* cause got attention, even among non-cyclists.[65]

At about the same time, the first American car maker came along, the Duryea Motor Wagon in 1893. The Good Roads Movement was growing, and it was big enough to get the attention of politicians. So Congress did something, and directed the secretary of agriculture to look into how roads might be improved. The Office of Road Inquiry was created in 1893. Roy Stone, Civil War veteran, retired general, and loud advocate for good roads, was the director. He called American

---

64   Grandin, 49, 24.

65   Swift, 14-15.

roads "the worst in the civilized world." Stone and his staff of two leaped to the fore when Rural Free Delivery was introduced in 1896, the Postal Service's caveat being that delivery was contingent on adequate roads. Again, a popular idea, especially in rural America, so roads were no longer the concern of only urban America.[66]

The Boonsborough Turnpike

The Boonsborough Turnpike ran from Hagerstown and Boonsboro, Maryland, and was the first macadam surface in the United States. In winter, stagecoaches took 5 to 7 hours of travel to cover 10 miles. (The art is by Carl Rakeman. https://www. fhwa.dot.gov/rakeman/index.htm)

It seems a historic and contemporaneous truism, that Americans loved gadgets and new technology. The fascination with new-fangled autos complemented turn-of-the-century politics. In 1900, Madison

---

66   Swift, 14-15.

Square Gardens hosted the nation's first auto show.[67] These political and mechanical impulses exacerbated the long-existing compulsion of a people inclined to move.

Horse sense?

Another national myth needs to be shunted aside in order to appreciate more deeply the appeal of roads and autos. Muddy roads were expensive to maintain. Horses were costly to stable and feed, and time-consuming to care for. Despite the later tales in movies and novels, travel by horse was not quick, nor easy, nor cheap. Ultimately, in cities especially, car shit was not a problem. About 8,000 autos were registered nationally in 1900, and there were nearly a million car registrations by 1912, almost double what they had been in 1910. A "good" road was a relative term at the turn of the century. With more than two million miles of state and county roads in 1909, only 8 percent were improved, only half that gravel, and a grand total of 9 miles being concrete. Automakers kept at it, creating better machines, faster and more reliable.[68] Cars and roads complemented the culture's nomadic gene in a way horses never could have.

Car sales accelerated in the first few decades of the twentieth century. Enthusiasm for the motor vehicles fueled a new kind of regionalism. A 1915 meeting in Chattanooga, Tennessee, attracted thousands of enthusiasts, and amid speeches, debates, bands and chaos, an organization called the Dixie Highway Association emerged, modeled loosely on the fairly recent Lincoln Highway Association and idea. The routes proposed were Detroit to Knoxville, and Chicago to Nashville, running parallel and connected in every state by additional

67   Swift, 16.

68   Swift, 29-30.

roads. The concept grew, further South and North, with the Atlanta *Constitution* even calling it the equivalent of ancient Rome's roads. Supportive groups—many private—popped up throughout the region, with proximity to the route no doubt fired by profit possibilities. Others were more idealistic, such as the Daughters of the Confederacy advocacy for a Jefferson Davis HighwayJ, traversing the continent from Washington, D.C., to San Francisco, via New Orleans. It was a clever concept for transporting not just people across the nation, but also carrying romanticized memories of the secessionist cause. The new roads were a mix of public and private interests, much promotion, some real pavement.[69]

Still, the existing roads were lousy. A State Department survey in the mid-1910s figured only China and Russia to have worse roads than America. For road-improvement advocates, the timing was good. It was not just the insult to being on par with the likes of Russia and China, but there was the reality that nearly 3.4 million autos were on roads in 1916, doubling the tally from 1914. The number would nearly double again by 1917. Nearly 80 percent of the world's auto were rumbling across and rutting America's dirt roads.[70] In perfect contrast to modern times, roads in the early 20th century followed the cars.

Progressivism and pavement

Early in the 20th century, Progressive Era road building reached its high point with the Lincoln Highway, conceived in the last year of Theodore Roosevelt's administration and finished—in very rough fashion—in 1913. It ran from New York City to San Francisco.

---

69   Swift, 19, 29, 44.

70   Swift, 47, 48.

Subsequent years saw it rerouted numerous times with a variety of changes to the paving.

Roads become an intrinsic part of the landscape with the commencement of the auto age in the early 20th century. By 1916, there were 2.3 million cars out there, with much mud, sand and gravel for travel outside cities. Roads became more than links to communities and became part of the landscape. There were only 387,000 miles of paved roads in 1921, and more than 2.5 million miles by 1960. While making the modern metro area possible, road builders were making escape from that same asphalt-and-concrete world possible, creating parkways that offered natural beauty and greenery.[71] Such a juxtaposition also created the path between two cherished national myths: the Edenic countryside, and city/land of opportunity.

In political culture, roads became a powerful entity unto themselves. State highway departments were cropping up across the country, as the federal government began in 1916 to put its own stamp on what many thought a local concern. A department devoted to highways was no longer an option in local, state or federal government. It was a necessity, practically and politically. Colorado claimed the first state highway commission, created by the legislature in 1909. Over the next few decades, the rest of the states came along, whether a case of popular demand or economic opportunity or both.

The various commissions and departments dedicated to roads eventually involved vast amounts of dollars, jobs, opportunities. All of these, in turn, invited corruption. Recall, for example, in more recent history, Alaska's "bridge to nowhere," which at a cost of nearly $400 million would connect a remote island to the mainland. The

---

71   Hindley, 111-113.

controversy began in 2006 with a national appropriation bill, strongly supported by Alaska Sen. Ted Stevens, and after nearly a decade of wrangling was finally cancelled in 2015. It would have been 1.7 miles long, nearly the length of the Golden Gate Bridge in San Francisco. However, the bridge to nowhere would connect the city of Ketchikan, of a little more than 8,000 people in the 2020 census, and its airport to Gravina Island and its 50 or so residents. Development was much of the rationale, as well as being more convenient than the ferry service. That such a project was even debated is testament to the centrality of roadways in our culture, not just their susceptibility to corruption. But, paved and unpaved, boondoggles permeate American politics, then and now. And roads are a good way to funnel money into states and communities. In general, we don't object to roads and bridges, let alone improving them, to some extent because facilitating motion is a virtue, then and now.

Once upon a time, roads were conduits of information. In the digital age, they are less so. Like culture, the uses of roads change—from carrying information and people and goods, to largely having the information function relegated to the digital world. This change has done nothing to lessen the significance of roads in our imaginations and daily practical uses. Early roads expedited travel into the frontier, and they still do—the frontiers of our imaginations.

Roads were critical to conveying the practical and the ephemeral. They separated wildness from civilization, and, as Turner proclaimed, that wildness was central to the idea of an American, whether or not a person actually abandoned civilization for the wilds. The frontier was beyond the road system, once upon a time. But in the 20th century, roads became a way to experience the frontier. The apparent contradiction—beyond civilization, but accessible for the summer sojourn—was ignored. And the "wilds" of national parks remained symbols of something very American. The frontier myth flourished along our roadsides and in souvenir shops.[72]

Though frontier came to mean a way of life, the place, real or imagined, remained at the very core of national individualism and exceptionalism. Earlier on, it meant crossing the Appalachians, and later was touted as a trait that made travel to the moon possible. New frontier, old frontier. The distinction was lost in the embrace of an experience, both historic and annual.

The Winston *Leader* in 1880 grasped the importance of the frontier idea: "A life in the open air, freedom from restraint, and a vigorous appetite, generally finding a hearty meal to satisfy it, make difficult a return to the humdrum of steady work and comparative respectability."[73] Though well before the time of paved roads and automobiles, the idea is as applicable to pavement and autos as to dirt paths and Conestoga wagons. If anything, we may be more frontier oriented than ever. We have more access to the idea, or the pseudo-experience, than ever.

In fact, our first "superhighway" owes its existence to wilderness, going through the Appalachians, i.e., taking people through what was the original American frontier. The 160-mile Penn Turnpike went through the Appalachians, and was simply a better road than the Lincoln Highway, which meandered around several mountainous terrains. The Penn Turnpike became a model of the interstate highway,

---

72   I have my own refrigerator magnets testifying to my conquest of the "last frontier" via the Alaska Highway, traversing such wilds as the northern Rocky Mountains, the Yukon Territory, and Alaska itself. All on pavement.

73   Winston (N.C.) *Leader*, August 24, 1880, cited in Grandin, 65.

as it went from near Harrisburg nearly to Pittsburg.[74] The four-lane, limited access highway officially opened in 1940, after more than two decades of planning, haggling, objections and promotions. Even in those early decades of the twentieth century, woodlands needed to be conquered.

Integrating the frontier spirit

Thomas McDonald, chief of Bureau of Public Roads, offered a vision of an integrated woods-and-nature highway. This came out of the 1930s, reflecting McDonald's admiration of Hitler's autobahn. Among things he found admirable about the German highway was the effort to integrate travel with natural beauty. The autobahns were consciously placed at certain high points so as to go through miles of woodland, even in the industrial Ruhr Valley. They provided views of fields, forests, streams, etc. The German system was tough to apply to America. The autobahn was built to a great extent for military purposes, not to serve population centers, and they were overbuilt for the volume of traffic.

This was contrary to McDonald's frugality, and probably to the politics of the day. In America, the thinking tended to be more purposeful—connect people and population centers, and provide better access to the centers and their markets for the rural populace. The German model stopped at the national borders. America obviously was quite different from Europe in terms of geography—borders at the oceans and only two other border countries, both quite friendly. And each was economic, as well as military, inferiors to the United States.[75]

Benton McKaye, a conservationist from New England, wrote in the *New Republic* in 1930 that green view-scapes and parks should

---

74 Swift, 132.

75 Swift, 120-21.

be part of the thinking about road development. Linking urban areas to surrounding smaller cities, roads would help alleviate congestion in major cities. He did not envision the modern suburb so much as a decentralized city. He advocated roads built for automobiles, not roads that were merely extensions of the older paths from the horse era. Just widening roads wasn't enough. They were crowded, with lots of sharp turns, and cluttered with roadside commerce, such as trinket peddlers and hot-dog delis. McKaye condemned them as "motor slums." He wanted horses and pedestrians out of the picture, and saw only gasoline stations and restaurants, which would serve motorists. He wanted to provide better views for motorists, one not tainted with billboards and advertisements.

This was the same person who conceived of the Appalachian Trail. Like his thinking about roads, the trail connected things, expedited travel, and gloried in the wilds. Perfect. He criticized the notion that a "modern" highway was simply better pavement, as opposed to gravel or dirt. Granted, they were better than the dirt horse trails upon which they often were built. Not only would the modern highway have fewer sharp corners, food shops, junk sellers, and billboards, it would be part of the natural landscape, like the Appalachian Trail. The idea even found life in roads built to and in national parks of the 1920s and 1930s, when the director of parks hired not only engineers to design the roads in scenic areas, but artists to see that the grand vistas in and around the parks were preserved and enhanced. [76]

This is an integrative ideal, making roads not just a route from point A to point B, but making them important entities unto

---

76   Swift, 106, 109; cites Benton McKaye, "The Townless Highway," *The New Republic*, March 12, 1930. The issue of roads and national parks is discussed at more length in Chapter 6, and in the documentary series by Ken Burns, "The National Parks: America's Best Idea," episode 4.

themselves, a part of a community, not merely an entrance and an exit. In this respect, the mythic road attained a new glow. One could see in McKaye's thinking the parallel to other ideals of American life—the skyscrapers that defined the might of the metropolis, or the green fields that accentuated the utopian, Edenic life in the country. Now, their connector—the highway—was endowed with a character, not just pavement, but something that integrated regions, lives and geography with wheels.

Even the term "freeway" is indicative of liberty—free from intersections, grades, factories, stores, and horses.[77] While the Appalachian Trail is a paean to frontier and frontiersmanship, the paved road is the new frontier. In this respect it is transitional—a culture moving away from horse and bicycle routes, and moving into the motor age. But it did not happen all at once. Even at this late date, more than a century after the beginning of the auto age, we are still enamored of horses and the romance of galloping across the Western landscape, nearly as much as we are of the imagined heroics of high-speed chases, cross-country truckers, NASCAR races, or the folk who decide to drive the continent, whether for a meditative sojourn, an escape, or just telling the rest of us to go to hell.

A new kind of frontiersman emerged in the 1930s, with the auto having arrived, as roads—good and bad—spider-webbed the continent. That new adventurer was the one-tenth of one percent of people who dared auto trips of more than 500 miles. According to surveys in the decade, people were using cars a lot, but most of those trips were less than 30 miles. Cars were getting better. They could go faster. That's what "better" meant. So roads needed to be better, not just in terms of

---

77   Swift, 110.

pavement, but straighter, allowing for speed. It was and is a national impulse to not just get there, but to get there fast. Speed is good, then and now, i.e., the popularity of car races, or looking at Mapquest to calculate the quickest route to one's destination. The impulse to move needed to be enhanced with these better roads, but also with fewer distractions. An "unobstructed view" usually meant a straighter road, unimpeded traveling, fewer roadside businesses.[78]

Post-war love of pavement

The post-WWII years were good ones for roads. Those years saw a boom in the auto market, cheap gasoline, and roomy cars well suited to going comfortably for long distances. The 1956 Federal Highway Act—and the attendant construction in interstates—fired the trend. Complementing the availability of autos and the burgeoning number of roads was increased attention to places where one might take leisure drives. By the 1970s, the National Park Service was controlling more than 30 million acres, with a lot of that having been designated federal forests or parks, including the Petrified Forest in Arizona, the Badlands of South Dakota, the North Cascades in Washington, the Canyonlands and the Capitol Reef, both in Utah.[79]

From 1945 to 1950, auto production increased about 60 percent in America.[80] It wasn't just the cars. There was more money and jobs in the booming industrial sector, and better roads accommodated new wealth of the rising middle-class. Autos, like homes in the suburbs, were a status symbol. The interstate system complemented it all.

---

78   Swift in ch.7 goes into great detail about the efforts to free roads of distractions; see especially, 116-118.

79   Malone and Etulain, 237.

80   Swift, 145-46.

Significantly, television was coming of age, and people had time and money for cinema. Westerns and romances were ever more popular. The road had not just users but an audience.

The presence of roads in cinema and television in the 1950s and 1960s was testament not only to their omnipresence in American life, but to the new growing sense of individual freedom and the demand to exercise it. Even before the war, the Joad family, in *The Grapes of Wrath* (1940), went down the highway to escape the dust bowl and poverty and then to return home. *The Wayward Bus* (1959) used the road to alter life itself for a salesman, an alcoholic woman, and a stripper. *The Long, Long Trailer* (1959) found two newlyweds at odds and with a road at the center of contention—he wanted to save to buy a house, and she wanted a mobile home, the freedom of the wheels. Even the convent found the contrarian in *Where Angels Go Trouble Follows!* (1968), when a young nun challenged the mother superior on a cross-country road trip. On television, all of America found out that *Route 66* was a metaphor for freedom and adventure in each of 116 episodes. Even now, that ramshackle route of diners and junk shops remains mythic. In both cinema and TV, it seemed police dramas required car chases.

Arguably, the idea of an interstate system was an old one by the 1950s, at least going back to the Lincoln Highway era. The first federal funds dedicated to the idea were in 1952, in the Truman administration. Though Eisenhower has gotten much credit for the interstate system, it was well on its way by the time he entered politics. As president, he did support it and move it along.[81]

Perhaps, in the wake of world war, overcoming a Great Depression, and taking on the Soviet Union, it was a good time to

---

81 Swift, 151-153.

project power, not just militarily, but culturally. Cars got bigger and faster, like American industry and the economy in general. If we could orbit the earth, then surely driving across the country could be everyman's aspiration. Gas was cheap; engines were big; cars more reliable; vacation time more liberal. Roads served this new notion of speed, power and freedom. What use was a 427-cubic inch engine on a busy city street? We needed a place to apply this new technology. The autos looked good, long and sleek, and roads needed to reflect that efficiency of design and purpose. It was American culture, on the move, looking ahead, and doing it fast.

The first superhighway, the 160-mile stretch over the Appalachians was, according to *Popular Mechanics*, "America's first highway on which full performance of today's automobiles can be realized." Initially, it was a toll road, a penny a mile, and the chief of the Bureau of Public Roads, Thomas McDonald, found this annoying. Roads were a right, as everyone had paid taxes on gasoline and tires, as well as state and federal taxes. His view is testament to popular attitudes about the right to unimpeded mobility. Not only that, but the idea of a toll road became less acceptable. Paying a toll was like a double taxation for doing what generations of Americans had always done— move. Whether of necessity or impulse was no one's business except the traveler. It was just what we did. Therefore, stay out of the way.[82]

Roads were no longer just a utility, an economic booster, or a facilitator of movement. They had come to embody—among other things—the ideals and national myths of egalitarianism, finding Eden, individualism, exceptionalism, and even rebellion.

---

82   Swift 132-135.

General Store

The ubiquitous roadside general store has become something of a forgotten sight, with the interstate conquest of much road travel. Now, these general stores are self-serve gas stations with mini-marts, inevitably at the entrance/exit ramps to interstates. (Painting by Jim Stovall)

Chapter 3

THE LINCOLN HIGHWAY: A SYMPTOM OF THE EMERGING MANIA

When the idea for a cross-country road came along, it was akin discovering the Mississippi River after purchasing a steamboat. The Lincoln Highway merits a chapter here not because such history is lacking, or even for the incredible obstacles overcome by the Lincoln Highway Association, including financial, political, and geographic. Such words are here because of what the highway and the push to build it reveal about the culture in which it was built. It was as much a triumph of imagination as it was of road improvements. It managed not only to traverse a very big continent, but it played artfully on the cultural impulses to motion, patriotism, freedom and exceptionalism. And never to be forgotten in any consideration of American values, it would make money for people. The project was aptly named for one of the great, maybe greatest, liberator of American history. This time, it was a different kind of liberation.83

In 1904, there already were 2.1 million miles of roads, according to one national "census" of roads, a measure that must have been approximate with a wide margin of error. Of those few million miles, only seven percent were deemed "improved," which at the time meant gravel, macadam or concrete. However, by 1903, the first transcontinental journey by car, San Francisco to New York, had occurred, taking only 52 days, with a lot of time devoted to car repairs and waiting for parts. 84

First, this is a story of conquest. We've all read and seen stories of "winning the West." This project is a real conquest of the West, traversing a vast continent, sometimes hostile in terms of geography and terrain, lots of sand, mud, mountains and skeptics, and even the most fiendish serpents confronted in such a project—hostile politicians. The idea that it was a conquest of sorts is accentuated by the fact that

---

83   On the history of the Lincoln Highway, see Earl Swift, *Big Roads: The Untold Story of the Engineers, Visionaries, and Trailblazers Who Created the American Superhighways,* especially Chapter 2, pp. 32-53, on the history of the Lincoln Highway (New York: Houghton Mifflin Harcourt, 2011). See also: Pete Davies, *American Road: The Story of an Epic Transcontinental Journey at the Dawn of the Motor Age* (New York: Henry Holt and Co., 2002); Drake Hokanson, *The Lincoln Highway: Main Street Across America* (Iowa City: University of Iowa Press, 1988); The Lincoln Highway Association, *The Lincoln Highway: The Story of a Crusade that Made Transportation History* (New York: Dodd Mean & Co., 1935).

84   Malone and Etulain, 40-41.

the military played a major role early in the highway, via the miles-long convoy in 1919, all the way from Washington, D.C., to San Francisco. It was post-war, so the rationale was there. People were buying cars, and they must have begun to appreciate the idea of a paved road, with long trips no longer being the domain of a limited number of auto aficionados and auto-travel daredevils.

The idea of a transcontinental highway arose as early as 1902. The Lincoln Highway was an ambitious plan, actually to build an "improved"—by the standards of the early 20th century—highway for automobiles. Cars had caught on with the public by the time a plan for a cross-country highway was announced in 1912. Though the timing for such a venture was good, it still would be a substantial achievement to do such a thing.

The urge to have a national road was nothing new, but coming on the heels of automotive innovation and availability definitely helped. As early as 1806, President Jefferson authorized building a national road, connecting Eastern port cities to the interior, and to be made of crushed stone. It was to run from Cumberland, Md., into Ohio and Indiana, the western frontier at the time. The road eventually ended in Vandalia, Ill. Despite the tribulations, the Lincoln Highway would become the first national road since the Revolutionary War.[85]

The Lincoln Highway Association

The genesis of the idea for the Lincoln Highway began with an individual nicknamed "Crazy Carl." Indianan Carl Fisher was an adventurer and auto lover. He was first to propose an "ocean-to-ocean highway," with suggestions for the route and how to fund it. He had

---

85   Hokansen, xvi.

been a car dealer, founder of the Prest-O-Lite headlight company, a great improvement over the earlier lard oil-kerosene lights. He was a partner in founding the Indianapolis Speedway, at first conceived as a proving ground for car manufacturers. His motives for advocating a cross-country road appear to have been mixed in that he had the economic interest, but he wanted to build such a road "before we're too old to enjoy it." He was an unlikely person for kick-starting such an endeavor. It wasn't just the skepticism that surrounded the idea for a cross-country road, but the fact that he was not particularly connected, politically, nor was he especially wealthy. However, his brash concept of a road from New York to San Francisco began to take shape when he founded what became the Lincoln Highway Association.[86]

The Lincoln Highway ultimately was a triumph of promotion and public relations, both essential to attaining such an expensive and ambitious project. The LHA's initial task was not so much the technical specifications or routing, but selling the idea. Among the first hires of the LHA was a part-time public relations man, and that was F.T. Grenell, city editor of the Detroit *Free Press*.[87]

The sale was best done on the basis of widely accepted, if unstated, values and myths. It was national, drawing on patriotic sentiments in the post-war years, and carrying the name of the Great Liberator helped not only with the idea of freedom, but gave an undefined, multifaceted plan a single, unitary definition. The president of the association wrote, "Here was a project big enough to stir the imagination and force the attention of a hitherto apathetic public.... The choice of the name gave a touch of sentiment and human appeal

---

86   Davies 12-14; Lincoln Highway Association, 1, 231.

87   Lincoln Highway Association, 27.

to a project hard as nails in its practical possibilities." In its own report,
the LHA said that it was formed not just to build a road, but to educate
people on the value of highways and stimulate interest in building
many roads.[88]

Even before there was an association, the person who would
be its first president wrote in the New York *Herald*: "The advent of
the gasoline motor has opened a new era and broadened the scope
of human ability [but] in America, the abominable road conditions
which generally prevail, both in cities and in the country, have been
and continue to be the chief handicap in the development of the home
industry."[89]

The car was new. The impulse to move was old. In this respect,
the auto was merely an accelerant for a pre-existing condition. Though
the Lincoln Highway encountered many obstacles and challenges in
conception and construction, it was rarely one of "why are you doing
this." That was a minority view. Even those who cold-shouldered
Fisher's idea, such as Henry Ford, did so on the basis of funding details
or the proposed route. It was not whether such a thing was even
practical or desirable. By the 1910s, touring had become a middle-
class activity, and, hence, demand for good roads became politically
feasible.[90] It wasn't just that cars were catching on with the public, but
more cars could be produced than the market could absorb—some
market hesitancy due, no doubt, to the fact that these new mechanical
marvels were restricted in where they could go. More and better roads

---

88   Lincoln Highway Association, 259-250, 252.

89   Davies, 25.

90   Howard Lawrence Preston, *Dirt Roads to Dixie: Accessibility and Modernization in the
     South, 1885-1935* (Knoxville: The University of Tennessee Press, 1991), 39.

would help. It was time for such highways. In 1914, for the first time, more cars were produced than wagons and carriages.[91]

The Progressive Era — Theodore Roosevelt (1901-09), William Howard Taft (1909-1913), Woodrow Wilson (1913-21) — correlated nicely with the appearance of cars and paved roads. It was even at the

The Lincoln Highway Association's ideas aren't dead. Publicizing roads and travel continues to be practiced by state and federal governments, and at the individual level. One can collect innumerable refrigerator magnets, as I have, going across America, in every state. Best of all are the bumper and windshield stickers pronouncing in a variety of ways, "I drove the Alaska Highway," some of them adding "both ways." The same things is available for innumerable destinations. It's not just a testament to good publicity, but revealing of ourselves that such pronouncements mean something, at least to the purchaser.

end of this period that the transcontinental Lincoln Highway was first traversed. At this time, the idea of interstate roads was taking shape, and became an important part of the political culture and government budgets, as well stoking people's wanderlust. The idea of a transcontinental highway came to bureaucratic life before motoring

---

91 Hokansen, 19.

across the country was feasible. In 1913, in Detroit, the LHA was incorporated with the president of the Packard Motor Company, Henry Joy, becoming the association president and Fisher one of its vice-presidents.[92]

Fisher understood the market facts and the American imagination. He pursued support from manufacturers. A notable exception was Henry Ford, who stubbornly insisted that highways should be built at taxpayer expense, not privately funded. Fisher needed Ford not just for financial support, but also because of his influence with the public and other car manufacturers. A breakthrough of sorts came in December 1912 when Joy pledged $150,000 for the project. Much more importantly, though, was the sentence that said, "Let good roads be built in the name of Lincoln." It struck a note for Fisher, who immediately saw a name for his project that was much better than the accurate but uninspiring "coast-to-coast" moniker. Now, there could be a name to complement the imaginations and ambitions of driving across America, a name that meant freedom, just like roads were supposed to do. At a meeting with Joy in April 1913, Fisher suggested the road be called the Lincoln Memorial Highway. The name would resonate with the public, a name with recognition, patriotism, and the sense of freedom. Joy liked the idea.[93]

The highway could be viewed as a triumph of commercialism and hucksterism. The LHA focused on promoting the highway, but it also needed money, as do most grandiose and noble ideas. The fiscally and politically astute board of directors was acutely aware that roads were "built of politics." It helped, too, that war-generated fear

---

92   Lincoln Highway Association, 44.

93   Hokansen 7-9; Davies, 25-26.

was an early inspiration for the road. It was akin, in this respect, to the next generation's Alaska Highway feat.[94] That was not to deny the Lincoln Highway's basic purpose and vision, in Joy's words: It was not the work of a year or a decade, but "the work of a generation." Joy did a good job on both fundraising and promotion. The association published guidebooks, garnered space in newspapers and magazines, and even made a documentary movie, which, by virtue of being a novel entertainment technology, would get attention no matter the quality. Like any practical politickers, the association produced pennants, lapel pins, stationary, and stickers. Clergy were even asked to sermonize on Lincoln on Nov. 2, 1913, the Sunday nearest a dedication ceremony.[95]

The LHA did not just build a road, though that took up a lot of its resources. It sold a road, or more accurately sold an idea. It did so in a way that made a cross-continent highway congruent with the ideals of democracy and egalitarianism, as well as commercial and economic growth. Joy grandiosely proclaimed this highway and others would do nothing less than unify the nation:

The national interest in good roads will continue to increase until we have in this country a road system second to none, which will bind this country closer together, eliminate sectionalism, eliminate provincialism, make Americans cosmopolitans, and work wonders in the unification of American sentiment and in the forming of a cohesive empire of democracy, indissolubly linked together through just such a system of highways as was the foundation of Rome's greatness.[96]

---

94 Lincoln Highway Association, 15; Joe McCarthy, "The Lincoln Highway," *American Heritage*, v. 25, no. 4, June 1974, 32-37, 89.

95 Davies 26-31, 69.

96 Lincoln Highway Association, 268.

It was a brilliant campaign in several respects, including the publication of a guidebook for cross-country travelers or wannabes. Even school children were drawn into the project. They were offered membership in the LHA for a penny contribution, getting certificates of membership in return. The fiscal return was insignificant, but the move produced a flood of human-interest stories, the association claiming those to be the best stories in the 20-year campaign.[97] It is not to diminish the task of the LHA to say that selling such a big, costly, even unlikely, idea could not have succeeded as well as it did without complementing and even expanding deep cultural values, i.e., a road for everyone, access to the garden/frontier, and a monument to the American spirit.

Routing was always contested, with various issues continuously putting kinks in the vision of a direct route across the nation. Those issues included the presumed benefits to local economies, good publicity for an emerging auto-tourism industry, politics and funding. The individuals who comprised the LHA had basically three considerations in determining the route of the highway: how to get most directly from New York to San Francisco; support from communities near the highway; proximity of the highway to scenic highlights and population centers. When the route was finally announced to the public in September 1913, it would cross 12 states. This came after considerable wrangling among board members, and among interested states, where governors and legislators quickly understood the dollars and political gains involved.[98]

---

97   Lincoln Highway Association, 120.

98   Hokanson, 12-15.

Cross country in 62 days

With the end of war and the availability of federal financial aid in 1916, it was time to sell the idea to everyone else. The LHA helped organize and promote a cross-country convoy with a large military presence to hype the highway. The federal government was amenable to such a trek, too, because it helped promote federal highway aid via the military and patriotism. A two-mile-long convoy of various military vehicles, including trucks, ambulances, and motorcycles, left Washington, D.C., on July 7, 1919, and arrived in San Francisco two months later on Sept. 7. It was notable not only for crossing the continent via motorized vehicles, but for surmounting innumerable obstacles, especially mud, with attendant repairs, and parades in towns through which the convoy passed. The convoy even had a 15-piece band in one of the trucks, perhaps anticipating the tedium and toil of such a journey. [99]

It was a great promotional device—what a way to combine the cultural impulse to move with love of new gadgets, a sense of can-do and conquest, all in the name of one of the greats in American history. With that all-knowing backward glance of which historians are so fond, the journey may have helped inspire and inform an individual who would become central to building the interstate system a few decades later. That was Lt. Col. Dwight D. Eisenhower, who joined the cavalcade at the last minute, having volunteered for the job. His later impact on the national highway system is somewhat exaggerated. He did not invent the idea of an interstate system, but he was there at the genesis of a cross-country road.

---

99   Lincoln Highway Association, 108-110; Hokansen, 84-85.

True to the political form, the endeavor was cast as an exercise in democracy. The editor of an Iowa newspaper, the *Carroll Herald*, called a cross-country trip "one of life's big experiences." He was a driver, having gone more than 700 miles on one trip, through much mud, contending with flat tires and narrow roads, and, naturally, finding himself in remote places with no safe haven for the night. Still, that sort of sojourn was "a sort of democratic undertaking, where the man in the Ford is as important and vested with the same right as the man in the Packard." The Lincoln Highway was not just an adventure; it was a leveler of possibilities that made such adventure more accessible to more people. It appealed not just to democratic instincts, but to that nomadic impulse that had so afflicted the populace from America's earliest days. Iowa was a good place to make the case. It was a prosperous farm state in the wake of the Great War, and it had the highest per capita rate of car ownership in the country—one in seven Iowans had an auto. Still, dirt roads were the norm, and Henry Joy created some acrimony when in a 1916 *Collier's* article he recalled his experience driving through the state in a wet spring. The place came to a standstill, with the deep mud causing schools to close and social interactions to cease, he reported, and cars became worthless.[100]

From the convoy's take-off point in Washington, D.C., the kickoff event to the endeavor included lots of speeches and ceremony. Even then, the question arose as to whether such a trip could be done. The continental traverse would be 3,242 miles. In addition to promoting autos and roads, it was a chance for the military to see what it could do with these relatively new machines. The highway was not finished by any means as myriad improvements were still to come,

---

100   Davies, 83, 104.

along with changes in the route, which often merged with existing highways. Still, a few wondered if such an endeavor was worth the cost. Most people had no need to drive to San Francisco.[101]

Now, of course, one need not take a band along for the ride, with car radios having filled the gap. The road has become a second home not only to radios, but for telephones and various satellite communications. The frontiersmen on the road need never lose touch with home and civilization. Radios, Bluetooth technology, global positioning, and the mobile internet make the solitary traveler an oxymoron.

A cultural marker

The highway was a historic accomplishment, but just as significant is its testament to the way in which the impulse to move complemented the emerging obsession with how to move—the automobile. Wrangling about the route of the highway only grew as the reality of the highway progressed, undergoing various route changes over the years. It originally ran through New York, New Jersey, Pennsylvania, Ohio, Indiana, Illinois, Iowa, Nebraska, Colorado, Wyoming, Utah, Nevada and California.

The road was not completed by the target date of 1915, but it was drivable in the summer months, the mud portions of the route having

---

101 Davies, 10.

become passable. It is in this context that the Lincoln Highway name and implications become even more important. With such a highway, even if one probably would never drive the whole thing, one might. The impossible was possible. It also became a proving ground for freedom and rights. For example, in 1916, two women rode motorcycles from New York to San Francisco, proving the fitness of women to be dispatch bearers in the event of war. The larger context was the enduring battle for women's rights, particularly the right to vote, which was achieved a few years later with ratification of the 19th Amendment.

Even in a semi-finished state, the Lincoln Highway attracted honeymooners, the military, the curious and the ambitious in towns along the route. The contention over the road's path meant bickering among various local and state governments, all of whom wanted the road but not the bill. It also was a modern incarnation of the "not-in-my-back-yard" types, people who wanted the business benefit of the road, but away from their personal dwellings. The Federal Aid Road Act of 1916 addressed some of the dissent, providing $75 million for rural post-road improvements, given to states on a matching-funds basis. Though little had been spent in previous years on roads, the 1916 act was part of another, major cultural shift. That was the way in which people looked at the federal government, accepting its role in road building. It was transitional in how people started to see government, vs. private or individual action. Who would own a road? A person or the people, via taxation?[102]

Up to this time, roads were local and state issues. Now, though, a bigger federal role was called upon. In some respects, such views of an active, even intrusive, federal government, presaged the huge role

---

102   Hokansen, 76-77, 83.

of the federal government in law enforcement during the Prohibition Era of the coming decades. In addition, the large role of a national government during the 1930s depression was not so new.

During the whole debate over funding and routing, popular support for the concept was out there. It was expensive, even invasive via the rights-of-ways that were needed, disruptive of traditional

---

Some of the questions that arose with the onset of the Lincoln Highway project resonate in my experience with cross-country sojourns. Friends ask, "Why are you doing that? Airplanes are a much better way to get to Fairbanks, or the Far West." They are right. I don't have a good answer. It's a genetic flaw. But even my personal head-shakers emit just a bit of grudging admiration, never absolute damnation.

---

ways. The immediate answer to such objections was utility. It would be quicker to get to town, and it would spur development and make some dollars. Just as importantly, one might go to a far-off place that previously was accessible only by books and newspapers. What had previously been all but imaginary for people, was now made possible, however improbable.

In 1914, the LHA produced the first *Complete Official Road Guide of the Lincoln Highway*. Perhaps it did for imaginations of those who would never traverse the road what *National Geographic* did later for far away and exotic lands and people. Most of us would never visit, say, Africa or Siberia. But one might go there someday. Road guides had appeared as early as 1901, many being quite abbreviated, little more than pamphlets of local routes—usually dirt. The *Official Automobile Blue Book*, at that early date, was mostly routes in the East. Only 19 years later, it had evolved to 13 volumes, covering the entire nation and much of Canada. It would be 1924 before Rand McNally published its first *Road Atlas*. The torrent of highway-map publishing is indicative of the degree of the fascination with travel, and a willingness to do so.[103]

It was reflective of a national mien. Something that barely existed at the turn of the century quickly became a presumed fact of American life, off-putting to those who lacked the modern byways. Frontiers became closer, independence was given new expression, and equality found a new doorway.

An egalitarian endeavor

By the mid-1920s, travel to remote parts of the country was no longer the domain of the privileged. Such ventures were becoming middle class, and grew with rising wages, along with cheaper, more reliable cars. Emancipating travel from rail and steamboat meant freedom was more affordable. Now it was possible, and safer, given the information in various guides, to take a family along. For individuals less inclined to a high-risk road venture, here was the way out and back home. That frontier spirit, and pretenders to it, was enhanced in road names, such as the Theodore Roosevelt, which connected Portland, Maine, to Portland, Oregon; or the Yellowstone Trail, from Boston to Seattle. You weren't just on a motorized jaunt. You were heading to the wilds, via a road named for America's cowboy president, or a

---

103   Lincoln Highway Association, 116; Hokansen, 85-90.

route named for one of the most magnificent of wild places on the continent.[104] The roads not only democratized travel, but adventure. All of the map publishing also meant one was more independent than before, when the river's course or the rail's route dictated travel. One only needed to know the destination, and perhaps not even that at times.

The LHA also accentuated, unintentionally but to good utility, our national garden myth when the association worked to get the highway outside business districts and municipalities. The utility was in expediting movement, not getting bogged down in slow-moving downtowns and the attendant distractions. Striving to move the highway to the countryside meant favoring the idea of the countryside as having intrinsic value over the cityscape. Another effect of such routing was to increase the dollar value of rural acreage.[105]

That a gaggle of individuals might band together to plot a paved east-west route across the continent of more than 3,000 miles must have sounded a bit outlandish, given the technology of the day, the money needed, practicalities such as land acquisition and routing, and simple shortcomings of the still new automotive technology, as well as unsettled considerations of what constituted the best pavement. However, these issues were subsumed before the larger context of American history and culture: motion and freedom; individuals and rights; frontier and conquest; the allure of new technology.

---

104 Hokansen, 95.

105 Lincoln Highway Association, 244, 258.

The Lincoln Highway Association

In July 1913, leaders in automotive and related interests began planning a national highway for cross-country travel. The group called itself the Lincoln Highway Association and launched a public relations campaign for national aid for roads. Work began on July 7, 1922, in Lake County, Indiana, south of Chicago. The painting depicts concrete paving of that section, completed in December 1916. (The art is by Carl Rakeman. https://www. fhwa.dot.gov/Interstate/artgallery.cfm)

Motion is freedom. The impulse to move precedes the country, even the colonies, itself. Sometimes it was less an impulse and more a necessity, such as fleeing the Irish potato famine of the 1830s. Still, it was a colony, then a country, created by people in motion, first from whatever the motherland might be, usually in Europe, then by the chance to go elsewhere in this new place. Imagine the shock of a peasant, recently arrived via Ellis Island, of finding that one might actually own property here, something unfathomable in the old world, given the dictates of class and geography.

Individual freedom is manifest in any number of ways, such as voting, or pursuing a livelihood or trade. It also is the right to leave one place for another, and to keep doing so. In that respect, motion became an important individual right. Having such a right, of course, did not mean it was easily actuated.

There was a frontier with which to contend, but one was at liberty to do so. Taking such action became part of the frontier myth, with attendant virtues of toughness and individualism. Roads facilitated forays into the continent's wilds, allowing one to participate in national mythology and history by striking out, down the road, across the country. Even now, lacking geographic frontiers, we still find a need to conquer those unexplored areas of outer space or larger democracy.

The freedom to move and the geographic obstacles are complemented naturally by love of new technology, such as railroads, telegraph, telephones, even weaponry. For example, steamboats only enhanced the romance of the great rivers, expediting the conquest of the continent and opening it up to so many more people. One of the nation's greatest writers, Samuel Clemens, aspired to being a paddle-wheeler captain before joining the ranks of the more mundane and less-heroic journalists and writers.[106]

Why build it?

In Europe, roads such as the Autobahn were built with purpose and destination. The same often was true in America. The Lincoln

---

106 A timeline of technologic innovations in America was accessed July 19, 2022, at: https://www.pbs.org/wgbh/americanexperience/features/telephone-technology-timeline/

Highway, though, was not born of such a practical and formulaic foundation. Much of the initial effort on behalf of the project was promotional, rather whimsical, in that there was purpose, but that purposefulness was bit fuzzy around the edges, other than getting from New York to San Francisco. Visionary? Perhaps. Practical? Not for most Americans. But it did offer an adventure, in the name of Lincoln and to a people devoted to motion.

It may speak to the power of the idea, or the intransigence of those who were pushing it, that the LHA resisted, and eventually rejected, pressure for rerouting the highway from President Woodrow Wilson, and from Sen. Warren Harding, who would become president.[107]

There was no single enumerated and named route, labeled "The Lincoln Highway." Instead, it was a conglomeration of numbered routes across the states. It was rather like the larger American culture, which was and is a conglomeration of many subcultures tenuously linked by the idea of America. Roads created yet another subculture in the national landscape of subcultures. The essential idea of the LHA—go across the country—eventually gave rise to "roadside America" on any number of roads and highways. By the 1930s and 1940s, roadside diners and gasoline stations were common, along with roadside camps of variable quality and amenities such as motels. Roadside America had arrived.[108]

The mid-1920s saw the practical demise of the Lincoln Highway as a result of the success in road building in general. By 1927 even the individuals responsible for the highway admitted it was "pretty well

---

107 Lincoln Highway Association, 160-161.

108 Hokansen, 116-122; Agee, 53-63, 172-177.

scrambled," having been replaced by various U.S. routes, numbered across the country. The New York *Times* lamented, "The traveler may shed tears as he drives the Lincoln Highway or dream dreams as he speeds over the Jefferson Highway, but how can he get a 'kick' out of 46 or 33 or 21?"[109]

There are markers and monuments for the Lincoln Highway. Henry Joy was commemorated with a monument placed appropriately at the point where the highway meets the continental divide, 194 miles west of Cheyenne, Wyoming. Even more appropriately, there are concrete markers along the highway. The two liberators are commemorated on the road. The highway itself included U.S. routes 30, 1, 50, and 40. Eventually, much of the route was U.S. 30. In the 1950s, the Lincoln Highway was largely replaced with Interstate 80, which even paved over some of the old Lincoln Highway, paralleling its predecessor in other places.[110]

Though the LHA would have favored re-numbering the existing routes, they knew the Lincoln Highway name had cachet. An editorial in the February 1926 issue of *The Lincoln Forum* reflected the issue:

The Lincoln Highway Association would have liked to have seen the Lincoln Highway designated as a United States route entirely across the continent and designated by a single numeral throughout its length. But it realized that this was only a sentimental consideration. ... The Lincoln Way is too firmly established upon the map of the United States and in the minds and hearts of the people as a great, useful and everlasting memorial to Abraham Lincoln to warrant any skepticism as to the attitude of those States crossed by the route. Those universally familiar red, white and blue

109 Davies, 222-223.

110 Hokansen, 114; Lincoln Highway Association, 217.

markers, in many states the first to be erected on any thru route, will never lose their significance or their place on America's first transcontinental road.[111]

The LHA's last official act was in September 1928, when Boy Scouts placed concrete markers along the highway and the association closed its Detroit offices. It ceased operations on Oct. 31, 1927. It had done its job, which was selling the idea and finding money for it. In its 14 years the association had raised about $1,250,000, much of it for promotion. By 1931, most of the highway was an improved road, thanks largely to federal dollars. Though the LHA was critical to getting the actual highway built, in one respect it may be viewed not as pushing something novel and radical, but paving the way, so to speak, for a value already deeply embedded in the national psyche—motion. The association did not just promote a route across America, but facilitated changes in roads across the nation, including improved paving, wider and straighter roads.[112] Such things are reflective not only of the culture enamored of motion, but of a people wanting to facilitate the motion— go faster, go further.

The Lincoln Highway Association was resurrected in 1992 with the purpose of preserving the original route, and, like the original association in the 1910s, hyping it.

Side effects—shoulders of culture's roads

A major accomplishment of the Lincoln Highway was standardized road markings and route designations.[113] It is a major

---

111   https://en.wikipedia.org/wiki/Lincoln_Highway#Lincoln_statues, accessed June 20, 2022.

112   Hokansen, 112, 113, 127.

113   Lincoln Highway Association, 210-224.

legacy to the extent that reliable signage and marking—such as the ubiquitous yellow and white lines—are as taken-for-granted as the pavement . Sometimes, the markings become part of the language itself, i.e., your own route 66, which means something to some people— perhaps personal discovery, or yearning for a lost past, an adventure, or paean to meandering. The marking also further democratized highway travel because one needn't be a geographer or reader of the stars to get across the country.

Even our forays into the so-called wilds of America are guided by reliable signage and, most of the way, neat yellow and white lines. Of course, in the early days of thinking about roads, such markings were a novel idea. The LHA 1916 report stated, "A mediocre road, perfectly marked, is preferable to a perfect road on which the traveller [sic] is always in doubt as to his direction." Imagine the direction dilemma of one traveler leaving Albuquerque who asked a reputable local fellow about the best route: "Follow this mountain range 80 miles south to a stick in the fork of the road with a paper tied at the top. Take the ruts that lead off to the right." Improved marking meant more travelers, of course, and in the case of one California highway that was calculated at 1,000 percent increase over two years after the introduction of better signage.[114]

Another major impact is the modern-day presumption that roads are paved. It is something of a novelty, maybe not welcome, to find that one is on a backroad of gravel. The LHA, in its own report, gave itself credit for popularizing pavement, of all sorts, over dirt. It is something of a turning point that people came to consider unpaved roads—

114 Lincoln Highway Association, 210-212.

such as gravel—to be difficult driving. Unsurfaced roads approached "impassibility" in the popular mind.[115]

Good roads, according to the LHA, had a social-leveling effect and reduced regionalism. The association, however, was perfectly wrong in claiming that cars and roads "made a nation of travelers out of the American people." It already was a nation of travelers, as discussed earlier. Undeniably, the cars and roads exacerbated the urge, increasing it in terms of distance and speeds unattainable in the past. There were, after all, roads before there was a country.[116]

Another major implication was the idea that roads should be straight and purposeful. Ridgelines or waterways were no longer adequate in the age of the auto. Roads did not need to just meander about the countryside. Roads were made to achieve a destination, specifically. It could retain its ethereal value, however. For example, the Lincoln Highway went from New York to San Francisco. But few drove the entire thing, using it instead for local utility, and if deciding to fulfill Hokansen's history of the Lincoln Highway bemoaned the coming of interstates, claiming the loss of the old routes in favor of interstates and speed meant: "If adventure is to be found along this Lincoln Highway, it will be found in the lives of the travelers, not on the highway itself." An arguable assertion. The road itself is an adventure, as one sees in a multitude of books, movies, and television programs, discussed later.

---

115 Lincoln Highway Association, 257-58.

116 Lincoln Highway Association, 263.

A romanticized road

The Lincoln Highway was a powerful symbol of liberation and possibilities, in much the same way, later in the century, John Glenn's orbiting of Earth was liberating. After all, what was the payoff for going in circles around the globe? Most would never do it—or drive cross continent, but now it was vicariously possible. The highway fired imaginations, set goals and aspirations that never even existed before. True liberation with autos was still a generation away, maybe more.

Break Time

The roadside diner, with the hamburger as king, has been a staple of road culture for decades. People gathered for food and conversation. Young people got their first jobs. Older folks, who weren't necessarily going anywhere, crowded in to see who else showed up. The coffee has always been fresh, just like it was yesterday and just like it will be tomorrow. (Painting by Jim Stovall)

Highway Gas

It was not just a gasoline station, but "highway" gas. And note the bench in front, where the traveler might cool his or her heels. An out-of-state plates undoubtedly provoked speculation and maybe even a query of the traveler. (Painting by Jim Stovall)

Chapter 4

INTERSTATES: THE DAMNABLE BLESSING

nterstate entrance ramps can be the access lanes to some national mythologies—the way to the frontier "out there," or the opportunity that must be greater a few states over, or the way for one to personally witness, even become part of, American exceptionalism. One even can do it solo, bursting familial or communal constraints, and putting an exclamation mark on individualism, or it can easily shift to a communal endeavor with family or friends. Significantly, such long journeys can be done more quickly than ever, not requiring one to leave a job or family, now being able to see America regularly and within the confines of annual vacation days.

Interstates are pervasive modes of travel in modern America, and too often have been maligned by those who inexplicably adore the rural route or the country crossroad. Interstates have made possible experiencing the national vision, the idea of America as more than an amalgamation of states, regions, communities. Interstates came of age in an era that offered a radical contrast to 21st-century politics. Post WWII America saw an enhanced sense of national unity, one in which the federal government could do good for people, and the idea of ownership by all could be a positive force, as in building a national highway system. It helped, no doubt, that the federal government largely footed the bill for such a gargantuan project. At the 1956 meeting of the American Association of State Highway Officials, the reception for Eisenhower's project was enthusiastic. The plan was for 41,000 miles of divided highways in 13 years, with the federal government paying about 90 percent of the cost. Though only about 1 percent of the nations' roads, interstates host nothing less than about a quarter of the approximately three trillion miles Americans travel annually. Perhaps those travelers forgot to read the authors who so revel in damning such freeways. Or maybe the travelers did not care about those opinions, having the more substantial endeavor before them of living the myths.[117]

However, it is hard to romanticize an interstate. For example, the Lincoln Highway carries the image of a heroic figure in our history, perhaps the savior of the nation. It is a line of federal, state and rural routes. The interstate, by contrast, strips away the risk, the novelty, the uncertainty of travel. It propels the traveler to his or her destination. Even in name, the bland but accurate moniker "interstate," enumerated

---

117　Tom Lewis, *Divided Highways: Building the Interstate Highway, Transforming American Life* (New York: Viking Penguin, 1997), 127; Swift, 318.

rather than named, conjures up nothing except a stretch of pavement. There is no deference to a state's imagined ideals, touted in mass-produced pamphlets and maps available at the borderline rest stops, where one can get the distance to the next attraction in the "great state of (fill in the blank)." Without even knowing the places and distances involved, there is a certain elan associated with the proclamation of traversing America via the Lincoln Highway, as opposed to a similar proclamation of having driven Interstate 80. Like history itself, the Lincoln Highway is subsumed by the present, eaten by current dictates and prejudices, and relegated to memory of a grand past.

The name, Lincoln, conjures up American history and freedom. I-80's designation reflects the brute, bureaucratic reality dedicated to purpose and trajectory, merely one number among many. Speed matters, too. With an interstate, one goes past places. With rural routes, one goes through places, i.e., towns and countryside. Romantics give little consideration to the fact that some of these faux Mayberries are best left behind, in favor of expedited travel, and predictable, clean, if boring, eateries.

What could take days on the Lincoln Highway, or even longer on rural routes, may be a matter of hours on an interstate. A common prejudice for the long hours between destinations often is a matter one seeing less of America's backside with the interstate. That is despite the fact that one might see more of the genuinely grandiose scenery by journeying more expeditiously to various corners of the continent. National parks are standouts in this respect, places such as Yellowstone, the Grand Canyon, and the Great Smoky Mountains. Granted, many visitors only get a passing glimpse of a larger expanse with a drive through the park, but even that would have been impossible a few generations ago, lacking a relatively quick, cheap way to get there.

Though roads in general facilitated freedom of motion, the interstates did so more effectively.

As early as 1965, when interstates were fairly new, there was a mixed response. *Time* magazine pointed out the "monotony" of such

First concrete road

Wayne County, Michigan, usually is credited with the first concrete road in the rural U.S. The one-mile section opened on July 4, 1909, to a festive atmosphere, drawing motorists, farmers, and other users. (The art is by Carl Rakeman.) https://www.fhwa.dot.gov/rakeman/index.htm)

highways, stretching "on and on." But it could benefit "leisurely and nostalgic souls who want to sample the color and culture of America's side roads...." There was a caveat: "In many parts of the country the building of a highway has about the same results upon vegetation and human structures as the passage of a tornado or the blast of an atom bomb."[118]

Interstates too often are criticized for degrading unique, local cultures, actually making the out-of-the-way peculiarities and charms of such communities too accessible and diluting them into a larger cultural homogenization. Such disdain presumes the regional had some sort of inherent value, something worth preserving. No doubt, building an aorta of pavement must do something in terms of sapping the life-flow of the local. The concern is irrelevant because change is inevitable, as is cultural change. Interstates helped grow local economies, which meant money for such amenities as education, housing, libraries, parks. Better access to farther-away places increased the horizons of opportunity, education, and imaginations of untold numbers of people, young and old, in subsequent generations.

The old trope of self-discovery may have been given new energy via interstates. One could tool across the country with fewer distractions, less attention to the local or regional sites and oddities. It became easier to tune out the rest of the world and turn the attention inward.

When one views roads as something more than paved paths, they become gates to ideas and possibilities. Displacing the county road with a cross-country interstate meant more freedom, more opportunity, not less. Interstates expedited the impulse to get in motion, see something, go somewhere else, if only for the hell of it. Interstates made individuals' worlds bigger. The presumed assault on local culture also presumed those residents were enamored of life in the hyper-local. If, for example, one believes the myth of American exceptionalism, then

---

118 *Time* magazine, "Ode to the Road," Sept. 10, 1965, 32-33.

one can better affirm it by seeing more of America and not hunkering down before the nightly news to take a network pundit's word for it. Interstates became critical to the road movie narrative. Anything that helped one move across the landscape could also speed up the narrative of the story. No getting stuck or slowed down along a few back roads. The narrative could take on the vast landscape of the nation itself. In many respects, the interstates revived the pioneer spirit.[119]

Interstates are used sometimes as a foil for romanticizing the forgotten out-of-the-way places. One seldom entertains the idea that such places may best be forgotten. Interstates did for physical travel what phones and, later, email did for communications—leveled the landscape, made the distant accessible. However, like social media, interstates simultaneously diminished and exacerbated regionalism and tribalism. Given the cultural panorama made possible by interstates, perhaps they have enhanced the tribal impulse. Disdaining interstates is testament to vanity, how much better it was "back then," a paean to what's not visible from the newest highway.

Opening up modern life loosened the confines of physical access, as well as fueling ambition and imagination. Like television, one might damn the interstates for cheapening access. The criticism doesn't bear sharp scrutiny because the interstate system also meant a larger world, for making different cultures more accessible, and one actually could witness, not just imagine, a nation large and diverse in landscape, ideas and people.

The romance of the past too often condemns interstate travel—and travelers—as losing contact with the landscape, whatever that means. The point of interstates never was to facilitate intimacy with the

---

119 See also Laderman, 38-41, on reinventing this spirit.

soil. Though the interstates sped one across the land, which was their purpose, the ideals of such things as individual freedom and equality may even have been enhanced. Like any road, interstates altered topography as they diminished geographic obstacles to travel. Thus, topography became not so much a challenge as scenery for travelers.

Some history

Interstates are not creatures of the'50s and the Eisenhower administration. In fact, interstates are based on older roads. They were no more an idea of post-WW II America than the impulse toward motion was a 20th century phenomenon. In this respect, the system is the modern manifestation of an older urge to go across the country. The first call for an actual transcontinental highway was earlier in the century, in 1912, when Carl Fisher was talking about a road—of rock, no less—from New York to California.[120]

In fact, the idea of coast-to-coast travel is centuries old, at least as far back as Jefferson's impulse to find out what he had bought with the Louisiana purchase and sent Lewis and Clark to find out, with the expectation of finding a waterway to the Pacific Ocean. That they did not find such a route did nothing to dampen the idea that a route to the West Coast would be there or be created. In the same fashion, the idea is even older than the republic, with the search for a "Northwest Passage," which was not there. Still, after much time, expenditure, lives lost, usually British in the earlier forays, the urge did not go away. Eventually, like good Americans, we created a Northwest Passage, of sorts, with the overland construction of the Alaska Highway, and then the interstate system.

---

120 Swift, 31.

Not even the interstate idea was a child of the '50s. For Eisenhower, it started in 1919 with the Lincoln Highway project. He heard of the army plan to drive a caravan of heavy military vehicles

---

It's called an "INTER-state," which it was in its inception, inasmuch as it was going to go across states. But like the larger culture, such ideals change and evolve. Some of the consequences were the growth of suburbs, fast-food access and exit ramps, of quick trips across town, of anything but interstate travel. My younger son, Robert, recalled a remark from a professor while Robert was graduate student at the University of Iowa in planning and transportation. He often went from Iowa City to Coralville, Iowa, on I-80, only a short jaunt. His professor noted that was not what the interstate system was for. But Robert rejoined with an answer, so quintessentially American, "So what? That's what it is used for." The professor missed the point—culturally, historically, economically. Robert did not.

---

coast to coast and volunteered to go along as a Tank Corps observer. Of the 72 vehicles in the parade, 65 were army trucks, with mechanics, engineers, medics, and observers. They did intend to promote the "Good Roads Movement," though, ostensibly, looking at the viability of long-distance trucking for the military, training people for a Motor Transport Corps, and testing equipment.[121]

However, it is not true that interstates were for military purposes. Some of the equipment could not make it under the overpasses. Federal Highway Administrator Frank Turner said it was for "goods movement," rather than troop movement. A related untruth is that the interstate system's intervals of straightaways was for sake of landing warplanes. The idea had not been ignored, but Turner looked at it early on, and said it would not work. They were for ground traffic. The straighter roads were often a side effect of massive land acquisitions for building the system. The earliest interstates took upwards of 750,000 pieces of property.[122]

As late as 1952, it still was a matter of federal vs. state government in building an interstate system. In that year, the first federal money for interstates was approved, $25 million for fiscal year 1954-55. It had been 12 years since Franklin Roosevelt appointed a committee to study cross-state highways. At the time, Eisenhower was busy elsewhere, drafting plans for the world war. All to say, he did not create the system. When he did take office as president, the interstate idea had already been in place for eight years.[123]

Debate over the interstate system focused on the impact on cities, not rural areas. In fact, Swift writes, there were issues for both areas, such as the exodus from cities into sprawling suburbs, and the attendant decline in the urban tax base. Farmland became more expensive, with each mile of interstate taking 30 to 40 acres of land, dividing contiguous farm acreage in the process. In Iowa, for example, 710 miles

---

121 Swift, 65-66. On Eisenhower and the interstate system, see ch. 10, esp. 157.

122 Swift, 223-224, 220.

123 Swift, 151-152, 157.

of interstate was estimated to use up 26,000 acres of farmland in the late 1950s and early 1960s. Such concern grew out of, and nurtured, the nation's garden myth by presuming a benefit to making countryside more accessible to more people, whether for living or simply motoring and vacationing.[124]

The impact of interstates was much more than simply cutting into and through a city. Beltways, bypasses and spurs came to define, and redefine, the cities, easing the way for new suburbs and business areas. In many cases, downtowns suffered while commuting exploded. Being outside the city even could be something of a status symbol as more affluent suburbs displaced the city neighborhoods. Sometimes, maybe oftentimes, cities came to be seen as obstacles to travel, and travelers could easily speed around the city. Speed was a virtue, anyway, and made more so with the bypass, i.e., better to go 70 mph around the city than only 50 mph through it, with the attendant risk, heaven forbid, of being slowed down by heavy traffic.

As for a city, Baltimore bard and culture cynic extraordinaire H.L. Mencken figured a highway through his city would win approval because it had "everything in its favor, including the fact that it is a completely idiotic undertaking." But it apparently was insufficiently idiotic because the proposal ultimately was rejected.[125]

The impact on cities and countryside was acknowledged by the more recent, four founding fathers of the interstate system.—Al Gore, Sr., Eisenhower, Frank Turner, Hale Boggs—at a 1996 dinner in Washington, D.C., to honor those founders and to celebrate the 40th anniversary of the interstate system. Various speeches acknowledged

---

124   Swift details the issues for each area in ch. 16 and 17, and p. 255.

125   Swift, 230.

that interstates had altered American culture by reducing distance and time between places, impacting urban growth, and traversing previously difficult, if not impassable, terrain such as swamps, bays and rivers.[126]

The "founding fathers" designation is, of course, debatable, but these individuals were important advocates with even more important legislative contributions at the national level. Eisenhower may receive outsize credit, but as president his ardent advocacy was critical, perhaps even decisive in getting the project moving. Albert Gore Sr. chaired the Senate Subcommittee on Roads and was critical of the proposal to reimburse for already constructed highways via bond financing. He deemed it a "screwy plan." In 1955, the Senate approved his alternative, which provided federal funds for interstates over a five-year period. The idea of federal funding, through many permutations, eventually became reality in the Federal Aid Highway Act of 1956. Working the shadows and largely forgotten was Frank Turner, the chief designer of the Eisenhower administration's plan for financing the interstate system. His career in road building spanned several decades and even included stints with the Alaska Highway in the 1940s and in rebuilding Philippine roads after WW II. He was the fount of technical information for Eisenhower's Advisory Committee on a National Highway Program, being very influential in committee discussions given the breadth and depth of his knowledge on the subject. Rep. Hale Boggs of Louisiana introduced what became the Highway Revenue Act of 1956. It provided that road-related taxes be used for highways, clearing the way for Congressional approval of interstate funding. Various funding proposals, via bonds and taxes, had been an impediment. But the idea of reserving road-related taxes for highways

---

126 Swift, 311-12. It is debatable as to who the founding fathers were.

meant motorists would be the direct beneficiaries of the taxes they paid.[127]

Community uniqueness was diminished, as local culture and quirks subsided, such as fast food replacing local diners. The thousands of miles of highways also made accessible grandiose parts of the American landscape that earlier generations would have known only via mass media or geography texts, if known at all.[128]

Invading Eden

The 1920s saw the first generation to mature without a frontier "out there" somewhere. However, increased urbanization and industrialization in that same generation fueled the need for a frontier, or the need for a substitute for one. It also was the decade of the Model T. Tourism boomed and was tied intimately to roads and autos. This, in turn, nurtured myths of independence and mobility. For example, one of the most striking aspects of the West is the distance involved, the space.[129] But autos and interstates shrunk this, if not in terms of actual distance at least in terms of time and expense getting there. In something of a contradiction, vast open spaces are accessible to more people, but at the same time have become less vast. Perhaps the reality of an unconquered frontier was diluted, but the idea was as intoxicating as ever. If anything, a vast wilderness as part of the nation became even more vibrant in the cultural imagination, as even more people could sample that wild area, or its remnants. They could even tout the achievement with a bumper sticker.

---

127 Swift, 165, 172-173, 177, 180-187.

128 Swift, 315-17.

129 Athearn, 65, 124.

Undoubtedly, the interstates did displace many of the old routes, but to bemoan such an effect is to miss the point of interstates, which were made for speed and facilitating motion. As seen in popular media, tourism and in the growth of national parks, to name a few, the highway is the adventure. The longer the traverse, the greater the adventure, i.e., one has done something to drive the Alaska Highway, versus, say, going from Tennessee to Kentucky.[130]

Such things as "roadside America," as has been noted in a previous chapter, were altered by interstates. Where the diners, gasoline stations and inns had tended to be local and individually owned, the interstates brought the chains, the corporations into the picture. The roadside was no longer Bubba's Diner but McDonald's. Character was not lost, but it was changed. Interstates were about movement, as opposed to the places to stop. It was no longer a matter of gawking at roadside oddities—such chain saw art or a garish sign hyping greasy food. Interstates imbued the road with greater purpose—get there, have a destination, have a purpose. Wallow in the culture of the destination, not the byways, which too frequently have little culture to speak of.

If anything, roads and interstates elevated the value and virtue of the "garden"— i.e., rural America—by simply increasing the value of rural land. Interstates facilitated the transition from city to rural by making suburbs more attractive and accessible. It was neither city nor country. It was a modification of the agrarian myth, which did not vanish. Still, the ideal lived for many of having a place in the country, beyond the suburbs. With suburbs—and interstates—it became a reasonable aspiration to leave the urban, and own a piece of land, one's own little Eden.

---

130 Hokansen, 131-134.

In similar fashion, ideas about the West are fluid. Once, all that open space was something to be corralled and civilized. As pavement replaced sand and sagebrush and crossed the mountains, the Great Plains were no longer a weeks-long obstacle of vast green but a long, even boring, drive. Main street curbs replaced the hitching posts, but only physically. The Western myth did not die with improved, paved access, no more than the ounce of whiskey on the saloon bar disappeared when water was added. The myth, the whiskey, is diluted and the volume greater.

More people than ever could discover a reborn American Eden, seeking the exceptionalism, individualism and frontier that had migrated to west of the Mississippi River. Though concrete and pavement may have replaced big skies and wilds, the obverse remained true in the national imagination.[131]

Frontier via pavement

The frontier lives in the national imagination, though its geographic reality has been diminished, perhaps even eradicated. But the idea has grown as more of its remnants were revealed to more people. Though the pavement may not take one to every corner of the continent, such remote places are within striking distance. The idea of the frontier is as strong as ever thanks in large part to an interstate system that allows so many to get to the faux wilds within the confines of annual vacation time and to do so relatively cheaply and quickly. One can get just a little closer to wild-place memorials such as national parks, which reinforce and recall the magnificence and bravado of the early explorers and settlers. Though saloon doors and hitching posts

131 See Athearn, ch. 4, "Eden is Jeopardized."

were inappropriate to interstate exits and drive-through fast-food windows, the pioneer ideal remained vital for those who might venture to far-off places with unfamiliar landscapes.

That the improved and ever-more intrusive road systems might threaten the uniquely "wild" character of the American West was not an idea new to the 1950s and the interstate system. It was a notion that started as early as the 1920s, with Eastern periodicals, which noted the increasing use of Eastern fashion among Western folks, similar attire from hats to suits and dresses to shoes. It was the same with roads. The frontier West was changing, though not suddenly and dramatically. It wasn't just access to remote areas and open ranges, which saw increasing amounts of barbed wire, or the small towns that were adopting more modern amenities. As early as the 1920s, there were those who begrudged the lurch toward modernization. There remained a push to keep a remote West open and green. Publishers such as the New York *Evening Post's* Oswald Garrison Villard complained that the faraway place was becoming a day's drive away.[132]

Undoubtedly, many Westerners like the idea and the image of people and place being an expanse of wilderness, not yet fully tamed to the civilities of the urban East. Yet, the tourism business, with its attendant dollars and monuments, has boomed now for more than a century.

Interstates only speeded up the fear of homogeneity. They did not create the trepidation. In fact, the push was about as old as the republic itself, as people moved across the dirt roads into and across the Appalachians, cleared the land, plowed the fields, raised families—to the ultimate detriment of native tribal ways and vast tracts of forest.

---

132 Athearn, 64-67.

The "modern wilderness"—an oxymoron?—became "natural and scenic, something to be looked at, traveled through, and enjoyed for its beauty," according to Robinson.[133] However, access, especially via roads, is largely to credit for redefining wilderness from "place" to idea, one that could be served up along the interstate, individually, selectively, and at one's leisure. Like stopping for the hamburger at a roadside eatery, whenever one pleased, and custom ordering the condiments. Now, national parks have taken the place of real wilderness, suggesting an adventure akin to watching a Yellowstone grizzly from behind the automobile windshield.

The idea of wilderness changed with the roads, the Great Smoky Mountains National Park in North Carolina and Tennessee being a prime example of such evolution. It is easily accessible via I-40. Gatlinburg, Tennessee, is especially noteworthy for its adoption of wilderness and mountain themes in order to promote tourism. More adventurous tourists discovered in the 1920s that their Model Ts could venture into the wilds, onto the area's log roads. Hotels followed and functioned as resorts as well as adopting rustic themes via the building of log cabins and stone chimneys. Being so accessible did not impede the allure of the wilderness patina. Even the residents of the area adapted to the new environs: Once, they had been semi-wild people; then, they were romanticized people of wilds; now, they are entertainment. Even the Appalachian Trail, a path of nearly 2,200 miles going from Georgia and Maine, had become a well-defined walking trail.[134]

---

133 Robinson, 114-115.

134 Claudette Stager and Martha Carver, *Looking Beyond the Highway: Dixie Roads and Culture* (Knoxville: University of Tennessee Press, 2006), 138-142.

Emphasis is on "idea." Note the adoption of frontier and wilderness themes to countless parks, towns and miscellaneous tourist traps in the West. Whether or not one has experienced a frontier is entirely debatable. Granted, it is more remote than, say, Times Square. Concede, too, that to 18th- and 19th-century generations, such modern roughing it—to steal from a title from Mark Twain—would be laughable.

Easy access had profound implications for the development of national parks as tourism shifted to more driving, making recreational motoring part of the formula. Still, the frontier could find a place to reside in the national imagination, no matter how far that might be from earlier concepts and experiences.[135]

Turner was concerned that increased access to and settling of the (imagined) frontier in the early 20th century meant a decline in the national spirit of adventure and individualism. It was a fear unrealized.[136] Imagine his agony had he any inkling of the pavement, autos and people to come. In fact, the roads and cars only dispersed the spirit, as more people than ever looked westward for an adventure, maybe with a car full of family, but definitely more daring than sitting in the front-porch rocker for a vacation. There came with it some sense of accomplishment, that one roamed the wide-open spaces, probably not on horseback, not living off buffalo, but "out," nevertheless, in a way previous generations had never experienced.

Yellowstone National Park is illustrative of Turner's concern, whether to justify or diminish it, depending on one's perspective. In 1917, cars replaced stagecoaches in the park. In 1920, the park logged

---

135 Stager and Carver, 259-64.

136 See Athearn 71-72, on Turner's concerns.

just under 80,000 visitors. By 1950, it was more than 1.1 million, more than doubling to nearly 2.3 million by 1970. It was nearly 4.9 million in 2021. Over that time, of course, visitation to all national parks increased. So it could be reasonably asked whether this increase in traffic meant the loss of wilderness, or that more people embraced and experienced more of America's natural wild lands.[137]

Often forgotten in the lamentations of a vanished wilderness is the fact that interstates, in particular, did not bring something new to the West or other areas that are now national parks. The change was already underway. Interstates speeded up the inevitable and made the places accessible to more people. The federal government, in a 1970 U.S. Department of Agriculture pamphlet, takes from Turner and credits wilderness with nothing less than shaping the national character. Because wilderness equaled individualism, regeneration, and a place to learn, it could not simply be abandoned, given up.[138]

Complementing myths

Opening up the country also meant affirming the myth of American exceptionalism. For example, consider the modern Alaska highway, at crossings in Montana and the Yukon, that has any number of trinket and gasoline stops offering up "I drove the Alaska highway" refrigerator magnets and bumper stickers. As though driving more than a thousand miles of paved road is an accomplishment, other than conquering the boredom that may overwhelm in parts of the plains of Alberta. But, admittedly, not many do it. If not ocean-to-ocean travel,

---

137　yellowstoneparknet.com, accessed August 27, 2022; nationalpark.com/yellowstone/visitation-statistics ; accessed August 27, 2022.

138　Robinson, 113-114.

interstates for most people at least meant venturing easily and regularly well beyond ancestral land and homes.

Interstates facilitated freedom by facilitating motion. Nationalism and westward expansion were part of the nation's founding myth, with expansion linked to democracy and freedom.[139] Interstates made the ideas bigger. There is nothing particularly new or novel about an interstate road. But the size, the immensity of the project—still ongoing—feeds the idea of American exceptionalism.

Interstates fueled expansion in post-WWII America by both reducing regionalism and tribalism and putting a spotlight on them. This contradiction is illustrated in places such as my home state of Tennessee, where one indulges in Appalachian culture via the crowds of tourist towns such as Gatlinburg, "authentic" country music in urban Nashville, etc. The regional is celebrated via renditions of imagined, romanticized pasts.

The idea of the frontier West was so enthralling that in 1922 even an Englishman on a visit to the U.S. found the isolated parks in the Colorado mountains thoroughly charming. He envisioned frontier vigor in run-down ranches with crude structures and scrap-wood fences. An American myth had migrated overseas.[140]

The Interstate: Its own culture

Interstates helped make roads invisible. One could be unaware of pavement beneath the wheels and totally reliant on it. Interstates facilitate the idea as well as the reality of people on their way somewhere, and fast. Motion is less constrained by place.

---

139 Robinson, 72-74.

140 Athearn, 73.

Like whitewall tires, side roads often were lost to expediency and speed. No doubt, the whitewalls looked better, a little classier, but the extra expense was in the light of a generation enamored of getting there, burning up the road. These were practical issues, and whitewalls, no matter how sporty, did not add to practical purposes, a critical aspect of American culture and technology. Considering the purpose of a road, interstates are almost beyond criticism for the simple fact of utility vs. imagination. Interstates enhance both. Interstates mean people can embrace the conflicting ideals of preservation and development. The highways make accessible the neo-wilderness areas of national parks, and simultaneously facilitate the journey to such places with easy access to fuel, fast food and lodging. Farms may fall to tract housing, but the local economy benefited. Even the ideal of a family farm was given vitality as the reality of development metastasizes. So often, something needed to be remote to be worthy of preservation. Remote did not necessarily have to mean difficult access.

But interstates, like roads in general, had the broader effect of amplifying our national mythologies. Opportunity, for example, was expedited and expanded by the interstates. One could go elsewhere, to the better job, quicker, and still be within a reasonable time of home, in many cases. Even if the time and distance were unreasonable, they still were doable.

Similarly, the Wild West myth, like other American mythologies, has persisted, and even grown, in spite of the fact there has been no such place for more than a century. Interstates did nothing to diminish it, and along with modern media, such as television and cinema, enlivened the idea. Visitors could witness it themselves, sort of, cheaply and quickly. If one wanted to see a shootout, Deadwood, S.D., had them on a daily basis during tourist season, featuring a faux Wild Bill Hickok.

Superhighways create their own climate, i.e., users and traffic, according to Swift.[141] To a great extent, they simply increase the intensity of the existing climate, one already enamored of speed and motion. Old ideals such as opportunity, equality, and freedom had found new expression on the road, and even faster expression on the interstate. Endowing aimlessness with meaning is often correlated, at least among the most privileged, with finding interstates a corrosive agent on the idea of community and values, forgetting that most Americans do not have time and resources—let alone an inclination—to meander the nation's sideroads. It is an anti-plebian implication that one ought to take state and county roads vs. interstates if one wants to "see" America.

In one particularly stark fashion, the interstate landscape migrated wholesale to the modern information highway, i.e., the internet. And that is the billboard, and their ubiquitous presence as one tools across the country. Now, like the highway billboard, one cannot avoid the e-billboards, often deemed home pages, in getting to the e-destination. Their ad-packed presence is simply taken in stride as part of the electronic landscape. Even the "superhighway" moniker was adopted for the internet as it became the "information superhighway."

Interstates expedited the idea that driving itself could be a goal, the accomplishment even measured thanks the advent of mile markers.

---

141 Swift, 136.

JS Market

Almost as predictable as the roadside store's gasoline pumps was the phone booth. Now a relic in the digital age, the phone booth was a sort of accent mark on the road as a communication corridor. (Painting by Jim Stovall)

Chapter 5

TO ENTERTAIN AND AFFIRM: POPULAR MEDIA ON THE ROAD

The traveler is a mainstay of American entertainment and media. He or she takes to the road, as well as rivers, paths, oceans, even airways, from frozen landscapes of the north country to near tropics of southernmost parts of the nation. Just like the audience. The paved possibilities are endless. That so many books, films, tv shows, magazines, even toys and artworks, are dedicated to roads and cars is testament to their significance in our culture and national imagination. This is not to mention, which I'm doing, the pervasiveness of mapping software in this digital era, in which you can hardly get a phone without the stuff. These and the old-fashioned atlases, city maps, and state maps—available in rest stops across America—are a different art form unto themselves. Levy asks if travel and roads reveal a lack of confidence in the nation's founding myths. But one might counter, don't travel and roads affirm and embolden faith in the founding myths, especially rebellion, equality, and individualism?[142]

Given the sweep of such writing and film, even a thousand-page bibliography would not do justice to the genre. For immediate purposes and practical considerations, only a few books, films and television shows have been selected to illustrate how myths work in media. And to annoy readers who will quickly find too many excellent books excluded, such as *Zen and the Art of Motorcycle Maintenance*, in which the author is on a quest of self-discovery, ala the protagonists of *Easy Rider*, the readers are right. There is no attempt to tout the few books, movies, and television shows here as representative of the expanse of road stories. Inasmuch as there is a mass-media road genre, it seems to be very broadly cast, as there are all sorts of episodes and words dedicated to travel. Much of the genre is travelogue, and much is dedicated to the mode of travel, especially the automobile, for which America has an undeniable love. But the focus here is much narrower, where the road itself is the story.

What may be most unique about many post-WWII books and films is the fact that motion is the story, regardless of destination or purpose. Character and purpose—if there are any—become secondary to simply going down the road. It is freedom, rebellion, individualism, all wrapped up in one. The plot enshrines motion, rather than a storybook ending, with destination incidental.

The popularity of road film and tv shows may be explained in part as a vicarious substitute for the real thing. One may not be able to

---

142 Levy, 238.

take on the continent via pavement, but those far-off places can still be seen and learned about second hand.

That impulse to meander even shows up in juvenile fiction, as early as 1852, in *Boy Hunters*, a title that would have different implications then and now. The author was Mayne Reid, and it was a favorite of no less than Theodore Roosevelt, who would become the nation's "cowboy president." The book was named for the three sons of a man who immigrated to America, and he sent the boys to procure the hide of a white buffalo, which they head west to find. Their traverse across the plains means much adventure—camping, hunting, near-fatal encounters with a bear, capture by Indians, who befriend them. They are eventually set free, kill the buffalo, and return heroically home. The father takes great pride in their journey and accomplishment. It is a travel adventure story, though lacking a proper road, as they roam and prove themselves in the process.[143] The tradition continued, entwining the journey and heroism, as exemplified in *Huck Finn*, who drifts down the river with his enslaved friend, to freedom. Huck is legally wrong and morally right. In the end, his journey continued, as he felt compelled to "light out" for the territories.

Modern roads, especially interstates, leave the aesthetics up to their inhabitants—i.e., of the automobile, whether a sedate family sedan or a sharp-finned '57 Chevy, the upscale Caddy or the workman's pickup, colors from drab gray to blood-red. Roads are practical and purposeful whereas the travelers may be starry-eyed and adrift. On the other hand, if one yearns for some purposelessness in a mission-laden life, the road can accommodate that, too. Paradoxically, one then needs to set and define the destination as nothingness.

143 Mayne Reid, *The Boy Hunters* (New York: Lasso Press, 2015 reprint of 1852 edition).

Though the travelogue has taken an interstellar path in more recent film fiction, such as *Star Wars*, the concern here is earthly highways, such as the likes of *Travels with Charley*, going down some good old American pavement. Intentionally excluded are car-chase dramas, which are standard fare for TV and cinema. The visuals, admittedly, are often very good, especially when wrecks, explosions and gunfire are added. Such fare has less to do with a road and journey and more to do with driver and car. Television police and crime shows would sputter and stall without high-speed chases and mean streets. There are exceptions. One early television series, *Route 66*, followed a few young men down the road as they found adventure and purpose along the way. The travel took them to purpose, and on a highway that is itself a national symbol, which no less than John Steinbeck anointed the "mother road" in the *Grapes of Wrath*.

In the first episode of the television show, "Black November," Route 66 has nothing to do with *Route 66*. It opens with the two young men going down a road, not really sure where they are, looking at a map, trying to get to Biloxi, Mississippi, and finding they have a river to cross. The ferryman tells them, "Nobody comes down that road." They do, of course, tooling down a ditch-riddled dirt road in their new Corvette, and having car trouble. They end up in the town of Garth, needing a mechanic. A man named Garth runs the town. Why are they there? In Biloxi, a friend "needs help. We need money." Still, why here? Why stop in Garth? "You live it the way you feel it," one of the young men responds. They are nearly lynched by a local mob, but escape, and they stop on the way out of town to say goodbye to a local maiden who had befriended them. Closing scene: They head down the road to freedom and adventure, apparently unavailable to those folks ensconced in Garth by lack of resources or lacking in the spirit of the road.

Like the continent and the roads that traverse it, road themes are pervasive in popular culture. When Willie Nelson goes "On the Road," there may be a destination, which is making music, but the road is the band's oxygen. And so it goes with road books and movies. The roads are usually liberating, replete with self-discovery, and even conquest, but there's no story without the highway.

Words on roads

Just as automobiles and pavement opened up a new era shortly after Turner proclaimed the closing of the frontier, so roads became the on-ramps to a new age of writing about traveling America. The first road book, in the modern sense of the word, appeared in 1903, Theodore Dreiser's *A Hoosier's Holiday*. In this respect the road was a new theme, just as automobiles and paved roads were new things. However, in another respect, it's nothing new, simply a continuation and enlargement of an old theme, and that is motion. Once upon a time, we moved on waterways and dirt roads. In the early 20th century, affordable autos and paved roads simply expedited the existing impulse to move. Dreiser's spawning of a subgenre in American literature in 1916 was followed by numerous road/car books in the 1920s and 1930s, though it was the 1950s before the term "road book" became widely used.[144]

James Agee cut to the essence of the issue in a 1934 article in *Fortune* magazine when he wrote that many Americans hit the road just for the hell of it. Later, a couple of notable illustrations of Agee's thesis are Larry McMurtry's *Roads: Driving America's Great Highways,* and

---

144 Douglas Brinkley, "The most American of American literary genres is nearly as old as the motorcar itself," *American Heritage*, 47:7, November 1996, 56-63.

Philip Caputo's *The Longest Road: Overland in Search of America, from Key West to the Arctic Ocean.*[145]

As noted, road and travel books—depending on how they are defined—are innumerable and could fill a substantial library, and excluding maps and atlases, histories of travel, such as Lewis and Clark. The genre ranges from the literary luminaries, i.e., Steinbeck, to the very plebian personal descriptions of local roads. Even more narrowly defining the genre as modern paved roads, the number remains suffocating. Just a quick-and-dirty Google search of "road books" yielded more 1.5 billion hits. Much of the genre is about autos and American culture. Both of which are relevant, but beyond the focus here on the road itself, and what it means in culture, i.e, the myth and meaning of the road.

Among the literati, Steinbeck's *Travels with Charley* is modern and artfully whimsical, though *Grapes of Wrath* may well qualify, too. Cormac McCarthy finds humanity's dark side in *The Road*. Jack Kerouac's classic *On the Road* endows pointlessness with meaning. William Least Heat Moon entered the pantheon of best sellers with the unlikely subject of *Blue Highways*, abandoning interstates and putting himself on the backroads of America.

When McMurtry said "My destination is also my route," he stated a cultural truism, whether in writing, moviemaking, music or any other appendage of popular expression. To his credit, he did not become misty eyed about the past when he stated that "place cannot be homogenized…," sounding as though he was looking at the roads constructively, not as a threat to an imaginary past. He caused consideration: Perhaps highways never were intended to homogenize or

---

145   Agee, 53-63, 172.

for homogenization even to be a by-product.[146] The national culture has never worked that way, i.e., thinking ahead. Instead, the highways are a route to appreciating or scorning the variety and diversity of American landscape and people. It could well be a point lost on the disdainers of the interstates, which allow more people to go further and faster. Not only do the highways let one bear witness to expanse of America and Americans, but they are actually an important part of the ever-evolving people and land. The highways are not just facilitators for the witnesses. These roads are part of the evolution of people and place.

McMurtry spent a lot of time generalizing about different states, cities, roads; with anecdotes such as neatness of Minnesota; or the number of '70s TV shows based in Minneapolis-St. Paul area. His history is brief and general, such as when he finds an inordinate number of serial killers hailed from the Midwest. As he divides the chapters city-to-city, stints of his trip, and the highways he's on that day, he merges mindset and landscape very imaginatively, going beyond the usual travelogue descriptions. As he journeys, he recalls literary monuments, such as Faulkner's Mississippi, or Ezra Pound and Idaho. The highways trigger thoughts pertinent to a particular road, but it is a path inevitably awash in discovery and re-discovery.[147]

In contrast to roads surrounded by meaning, Jack Kerouac's *On the Road* makes the road itself meaningful. Travel is the plot, with no apparent values at issue. His protagonists seem to be rebels, but it is unclear what they are rebelling against. The road facilitates their brand of hedonism. Kerouac's literary legacy may have been forever stained by

---

146 Larry McMurtry, *Roads: Driving America's Great Highways* (New York: Simon and Schuster, 2000), 12, 16.

147 McMurtry, 39, 61. See 194-195 on Idaho and Ezra Pound, Ernest Hemingway and literary lights.

Truman Capote's quip "that's not writing. It's typing." He may be right, but writing starts with typing, just as Kerouac's self-discovery begins with the road, just as any journey begins with fueling up. That's not traveling, that's driving. The quality of the writing may be debatable, but Kerouac got there first.[148]

Similarly, in *The Electric Kool-Aid Acid Test*, by Tom Wolfe, a gaggle of hippies gad about rebelliously, flouting the establishment, going around the country in a painted bus, via their industrial machine, via communally funded roads of "the establishment."

The road isn't always a lark. Cormac McCarthy's *The Road* is a tale in which the journey is the point of the story. The point may be that it is not the destination but the journey. The father-and-son travelers do make a discovery, about the dark side of life's journey. In the same way, stories of 19th-century westward travelers are seldom about the fact that they find a place to farm or establish a general store. The adventure is in getting there. There are few dramatic Westerns about farming and plowing, compared to wagon trains, lone horsemen, cowboys, the trail, etc.

The modern-day cowboy hits the trail again, this time paved, with Lee Child's "Jack Reacher" novels. The loner, Reacher wanders into town, from nowhere in particular, often on a bus, thrashes the bad guys, never for reward, only for the sake of doing what's right. Then back out of town and down the road, on a bus or with thumb out for a ride. For example, in *Nothing to Lose,* Reacher is walking and hitchhiking from Maine to California. He gets caught up in factory-town corruption, and so goes back and forth between the aptly named

---

148 The Capote quip appeared in the 1957 spring-summer issue of *The Paris Review*. It was the apparent earliest version of the quip. Several more appear later in the 1950s.

Western towns of Hope and Despair. The road to Hope, by the way, is much better pavement than the road to Despair, which in only tar and gravel. In *Blue Moon*, Reacher first appears on a bus, deters a mugger in the first two chapters, tells the aged couple he's saving from financial disaster that he'll be moving on soon, and he leaves town on a bus, "drifting north for the summer." A novel's movie version, *Jack Reacher*, has the protagonist, a loner, showing up out of nowhere. He tells the attractive, female assistant district attorney who he is helping, "I'm a drifter with nothing to lose…." Again, he rescues a damsel in distress, and in the final scene, he leaves town on a bus, destination unknown. As the bus heads down the road, a brouhaha breaks out, with a man abusing a woman. So Reacher walks to the disturbance, and the film ends. It is the wandering cowboy, on a bus instead of horse.

The literature often finds roads to be a means of escape, such as Oakies fleeing the depression-era dustbowl, or bemoaning something lost, such a local color. But that needs to be weighed against the promise of the road. The Oakies' road, in *The Grapes of Wrath*, is a route to something more, a promise, but when that fizzles, the road goes back home. It is triumphal.

James Joyce's Leopold Bloom illuminates, but does not answer, the dilemma, when he asks in *Ulysses* if it is the road that creates the traffic or vice versa. And so goes the road in literature—a way out, a way in. It goes somewhere. It goes nowhere. [149]

A driven industry

More and better roads meant the film industry would discover the West along with the rest of America, at least for those who did

---

149 Joyce is quoted in Levy, 18.

not already reside in it. The West was a grand staging area for movie making, and the region's lore and highways were conducive to cinematic story telling.[150]

Bridge to Somewhere
In the mid-1800's, proposals for bay crossings included both road and railway bridges. After ground was broken for the San Francisco-Oakland Bay Bridge in July 1933, the project was finished forty months later. (The painting is by Carl Rakeman. https://www.fhwa.dot.gov/Interstate/artgallery.cfm)

It is hard to separate the road film from the car film, given the symbiotic relationship of roads and cars. The very few movies discussed here are selected for the emphasis not so much on cars or car crashes as for emphasis on a journey, on the pavement. The means for making the

---

150 Malone and Etulain, 46-47.

journey obviously is the auto, which is necessarily the focus of many stories, as it might be in Ron Howard's directorial debut *Grand Theft Auto* (1977), or in which the chase is the story, i.e., *Smokey and the Bandit* (1983).

First among post-WWII road movies is *Easy Rider*. The protagonists meander down the road, like so many Western-genre cowboys who often just ride off into the sunset, leaving any heroism behind. The ostensible purpose of the easy riders is to sell drugs. The road is freedom, but it can be dangerous, as in the ending, where Billy gives the finger to man in pickup with shotgun and pays the price. His life. When Captain America speeds off the scene of the shooting to get help for Billy, he too pays the price. The road is life and death for them. Like the drug dealers it elevates to near-heroic status, the movie made a lot of money, too. It cost $400,000 to make, and eventually grossed about $30 million.[151]

Jack Nicholson wrote the script. Dennis Hopper and Peter Fonda were the stars. It was not just a rebellion from place, but also from financial norms: Selling drugs was their road to the American dream. Unlike *Route 66*, they do have a way of making money. And unlike *Route 66*, they are on less conventional vehicles, the motorcycles, often seen as devices for people who menace society, i.e., Hells Angels, made into counterculture heroes a few years earlier by Hunter Thompson' in *Hells Angels: The Strange and Terrible Saga of the Outlaw Motorcycle Gang*, which affirmed the role of motorcycling down the road as a counterculture.[152]

---

151 Katie Mills, *The Road Story and the Rebel: Moving Through Film, Fiction and Television* (Carbondale: Southern Illinois University Press, 2006), 126-127.

152 Mills,123.

Easy Rider starts with drug dealing in a ramshackle Mexican junkyard, buying drugs to resell. About five minutes into the film, Captain America (Peter Fonda) takes off his wristwatch and throws it into dust, to the soundtrack of Steppenwolf's "Born to be Wild." About 30 minutes in they stop in a dusty commune, populated with a small group of "city kids," deemed so by their traveling companion. Later, George Hanson (Jack Nicholson) with college sweatshirt on that evening, launches into a monologue on UFOs, their inhabitants, etc. When they stop in a small-town cafe, they can't get waited on. Hanson tells Billy and Captain America the townspeople fear what the duo represents, and that is freedom. The pair are, according to Hanson, "dangerous." That night, the three of them are visited by a group, apparently townsmen, who beat them with sticks, killing Hanson. Billy and Captain America make it to Mardi Gras, visit a brothel, get drunk and high. Near the end, Billy proclaims, "We're rich." He says you go for big money, and you are free. It is a very down-to-earth Horatio Alger story. Granted that, in *Easy Rider*, Captain America and Billy are in search of "something," presumably giving them some deeper meaning beyond the moment. When they are killed at the end, the final scene being Captain America's exploding motorcycle, it is not only that they lived in motion, but they died in motion, on the road. It is in sync with the zeitgeist of the 1960s: If you can't be heroic—or don't want to be—then be rebellious. The road is a good way to do that, freeing one from place, purpose, even other people.

Easy Rider is a hippie film about finding oneself. Even though the protagonists have long hair and are rebels, they are the antithesis of the '60s counterculture in that they are out to make money. So it's extremely rebellious, no one matters but themselves. It's anti-culture and anti-counterculture. It is purest rebellion, i.e., rebelling again rebellion. Still, it's an American myth. Rebellion is tied to the Horatio Alger dream of making money, but not done in conventional fashion. The road makes fulfillment of the dream possible.

In this film, there is an aura, a sexual mystique, about the travelers. It is shown with the females attracted to Billy and Captain America when they stop at the commune and take a nude dip with two of the female inhabitants. At the small-town café, a booth full of teenage girls start giggling and flirting with them, rousing the ire of some local male diners,. The rebels are sexy, the mysterious wanderers, ala the horseman of the Western genre.[153]

That sort of sexual aura comes more to the fore, but still implicit rather than explicit, in *Bonnie and Clyde*. The couple leave home and convention, unmarried. *Bonnie and Clyde* came out about two years before *Easy Rider*, the former in the more traditional, studio tradition of moviemaking, the latter an independent, with unconventional filming and editing, as well as less conventional protagonists. Despite the sharp contrasts in style, rebellion and Horatio Alger myths are central to each. Like the protagonists in *Easy Rider*, Clyde wants money. *Bonnie and Clyde* steal the money. So the American dream finds new expression on the road. It is the quest for money that keeps the protagonists in both movies recognizable in the context of American myths. In both movies the road liberates the protagonists from convention, but not from a capitalist goal.[154]

Both movies are examples of films in which the road is the story, i.e., there is no story without it. In addition, they profit from just going down the road. Too, both *Bonnie and Clyde* and *Easy Rider* are

---

153 Laderman, 72.

154 Laderman, 64.

buddy movies, putting them in a tradition of movie making, especially reminiscent of Westerns. Both movies are anti-social, with gangsters as heroes in one, long-haired, drug-using hippies in the other.[155] In each case, the rebels pay the price. Bonnie and Clyde die when the motion stops.

Some sort of purposelessness prevails in each, the easy riders have no professed purpose ahead of them other than drug money. In *Bonnie and Clyde*, the point is simply to go down the road and rob banks. This frustrates Bonnie, who at one point says, "… I thought we were really goin' somewhere. But this is it. We're just goin'." In this respect *Easy Rider* more explicitly celebrates the road than *Bonnie and Clyde*.[156]

In a 1991 movie, *Thelma and Louise*, the road is independence and empowerment for two women. *Thelma and Louise* take control of their fates when they trade home for the highway, leaving a bad marriage and a mundane relationship, even sleeping in a motor inn, where social norms are discarded, and adultery takes on an aura of ennobling rebellion. When they fire away at a male trucker who insulted them on the road, the women reverse the usual roles of power. The driver of the big rig cowers before them. On this road, two women prevail. In the course of their travel, one murders a would-be rapist, and they rob a convenience store. They violate more sexual norms when, at the end, they hold hands and kiss. Then, they decide to flee one last time—to their demise—when they are cornered by police. It may be the purest rebellion against society when they abandon the pavement, leaving the road and driving off a cliff.

---

155 Laderman, 67; Mills, 137-139.

156 Laderman, 56, 70-71.

According to Laderman, there are primarily two narratives in the road genre: The quest movie and the outlaw movie. *Bonnie and Clyde* is clearly the latter, but the two narrative types overlap. *Easy Rider* has the outlaw element, though the quest seems primary. Similarly, *Bonnie and Clyde* has some element of self-discovery.[157]

More purely in the quest vein, and more recently, *Nomadland* (2020) lent a certain dignity to the plight of people uprooted, living in campers and recreational vehicles, unemployed and surviving on seasonal work, but of a community invisible to the rest of America. The life is difficult, not so romantic. Nevertheless, they persevere, strike their own way, endure and move. The protagonist is a woman in her 60s, who loses her job, and is forced out of her home. This after a lifetime of low-income jobs. When she takes to the road with a small trailer, it is a matter of survival, which is her destination. Other than food and shelter, she now just needs a road and a vehicle. Unlike earlier films, the road is no longer a lark, but a purpose in and of itself.

The movie is an adaptation of a 2017 book of the same name. In the book and movie, however, the road becomes a place of hope. It still is an escape from convention, from the long-time neighborhood. But the road offers the chance to become part of another community. The aspiration is simply self-sufficiency. She attains this in a way, tenuously, but on her own. It is in a tradition of American individualism, as she finds independence and a community.

The road movies say something about the limits of the myth of individualism: The pavement is the limit. Though road movies often are about freedom and rebellion, one is limited in direction and destination, confined to the white lines along the shoulders. The only

---

157 Laderman, 20.

way off is death, as in the end of *Thelma and Louise*, *Easy Rider*, and *Bonnie and Clyde*. So the irony of rebellion via the road is the fact that it is done within the confines of the socially constructed path of pavement.[158]

On the small screen, *Route 66* was one of the earliest television road shows, premiering in 1960 and running for four seasons. Each weekly episode was filmed in a different town, making the road an adventure, a moral one at that, done with two handsome, wholesome young men. Not to say they were not rebels. They are outcasts of a privileged sort, unlike Captain America and Billy in *Easy Rider*. But *Route 66's* protagonists were a new take on traditional rebels. They are wandering but the object of rebellion is unclear. They appear unattached to a place, except the car and the road. They drive a Corvette, which means power, but the issue of economics never arises, how they could afford such pricey wheels. It is a story about freedom, from place apparently, but also social norms, such as having a job, and the norms of behavior between men and women.[159]

It's a contrast to the Charles Kuralt-style travelogue. His very popular *On the Road* ran on CBS from 1967 to 1980, with Kuralt logging more than a million miles over the years and wearing out several mobile homes as he ran the backroads and shunned the interstates. He was looking for, maybe even finding, America along the roads. Here was a news feature that gloried in the road as a gateway to a nation of unique people and places. In the process of cataloguing the country, certain cultural constants came to the fore time and again in the people and places he visited, usually implicitly, sometimes explicitly:

---

158 Laderman touches on this idea, 2.

159 Mills,75, 11.

individualism, exceptionalism, the promise of the frontier, the rebel, and egalitarianism, to name a few.

Kuralt disdained the interstates. His subjects ranged from horse traders to lobster fishermen to migrant workers. In the first episode, he comes across a 104-year-old man whose longevity secret is staying active. In fact, he challenged Kuralt to a foot race. The old man won, and so did CBS' ratings with the series. In another episode, Kuralt featured an impoverished black family in rural Mississippi who put nine children through college. His road stories highlighted America as a land of opportunity and exceptionalism, studying those common people of uncommon accomplishment, even if it had to be divined by Kuralt. He wrote several books, including *On the Road with Charles Kuralt"* (1985), *Charles Kuralt's America* (1995), *Dateline America* (1979), and *A Life on the Road,* (1990), his autobiography.

The road, though, ultimately revealed something more about Kuralt, and that was a whole different life. His wife and two daughters resided in in Manhattan. But after his death in 1997, a second life came to light. He had a lover in San Francisco, so a court battle ensued over his property in Montana, with a house near the Big Hole River, where he loved trout fishing. His mistress eventually won the property. The road made such a double life possible. In effect, he led three lives: in Manhattan, in Montana, and on the road.

Perhaps most significantly, *On the Road* and its huge audience affirmed the importance and the love of motion. Oftentimes, the purpose was little more than finding the next oddity down the road. For the audience, it was the vicarious thrill of finding America from the comfort of the sofa, knowing it was out there and accessible if one had to urge to hit the road.

The road show is not lost to modern television. Illustrating the road as taken for granted, presumed, and critical to the subject at hand, there is Ken Burns' PBS series *The National Parks: America's Best Idea* (2009), which notes that the parks were created and preserved for everyone, and even devotes some time to individuals who have visited all of the of the roughly sixty parks—numbers vary and grow over time. The endeavor is heroic, and not possible without the roads from one place to another but also the roads inside the parks. With these people, it is not just the destination, but the roads themselves that are the frontier to be conquered. Just as the old West could not have been settled without horses, the modern park system ultimately required auto and road. It probably is not impressive that one visited Yellowstone or the Grand Canyon or Denali. It is an attention grabber if one did so by automobile. In fact, the first director of the national park system, advocated cars and roads in the parks as a means of creating public support. He was right.[160]

In a three-part series with a slightly different twist to the travelogue, a Muslim couple, in *The Great American Muslim Road Trip*, take a trip down Route 66 and visit Muslim communities from Chicago to Los Angeles. It is a discovery story, true to the genre, but one of a religion's roots in America and its contributions to the larger culture.

The road was then, and continues to be, a place of adventure, romance and discovery.

---

160 Ken Burns *The National Parks: America's Best Idea*, part four, "Going Home."

Going somewhere

Roads amplify our myths like a car without a muffler exaggerates the noise of the engine.

A myth should be purposeful, just as road should have a destination, like a good story. Otherwise, one is merely a tramp, wandering and aimless. Destination commonly presumes a geographic point. The road might be a route to justice, as in the Jack Reacher novels. But cars and roads have broadened the idea to the point that driving itself may be the goal, a form of recreation and entertainment, a sort of therapy. Or the use may be more mundane, such as finding out your car's highway mileage vs. city mileage. More ethereally, the purpose might be wrapped in a myth, such as finding that Edenic garden. Or one simply can be rebellious for the hell of it. It's easy enough to accomplish with modern roads and autos. Think *Route* 66 or *Easy Rider*.

The Wild West myth affected much writing about the region, fiction and non-fiction. Writers focused on conflict, which was a more dramatic and interesting story than yoked oxen plodding across or plowing the prairie. Such romanticism is reflected, too, in road building, an expensive, communal task at best, not usually a good story of conquest. There were more dissenters, such as Bernard DeVoto, who saw not triumph in the Western saga, but a region still in the grip of Eastern money and political interests.[161] The more accurate story may not be in the conquest with six-gun, but the reality of the conquering that great expanse with the road, which was the most significant force in civilizing wild areas.

---

161 Malone and Etulain, 174-173.

That lone cowboy of much pulp fiction and B movies could be anyone with car and gas money. It's possible to travel coast to coast and not speak to anyone, thanks to credit cards. The Beats of the 1950s and 1960s amplified several values, and two things in particular that made a mark on subsequent road literature. First, optimism: the road as freedom; two, rebellion via the road. Maybe the greatest accomplishment and legacy of the Beats was to endow meaninglessness with meaning. With them, the road became the meaning, values and mores be damned. The road offered redemption.[162]

Of course, the road does go someplace, though its traveler may have none in mind. In neither fact nor story-telling fantasy do roads need destinations. Roads fire restless spirits. Agee got it when he wrote that "God made the American Restive." "The American in turn and in due time got the automobile and found it good. The war exasperated his restiveness, and the twenties made him rich and more restive still and he found the automobile not merely good but better and better. It was good because continuously it satisfied and at the same time greatly sharpened his hunger for movement...." A Flannery O'Connor character states: "The body, lady, is like a house: it don't go anywhere; but the spirit, lady, is like an automobile: always on the move always."[163]

Roads often are thought to be paved paths to convenience, reinforcing cultural norms. But those highways are just as often an escape route, not just from the daily grind but from life itself. We find on them the American rebel, the entrepreneurial spirit, an escape to Eden, and freedom, even from life itself.

---

162   Mills, 41.

163   The Agee article is cited in the Brinkley article, as well as the O'Connor short story, "The Life You Save May Be Your Own."

Whitewalls

Whitewall tires were a second-generation invention, and like the sporty cars of the '50s and '60s were an adornment to the institution of auto-art and its aorta, the highway. Like much in American culture, the whitewalls eventually succumbed to practicality and new trends in auto fashion, such as mag wheels. Autos had fins and whitewalls. Roads had, and still have, the scenic route. (Painting by Jim Stovall)

Conclusion:

Some Roads Never End

ociety's penchant for pavement exists in both fact and in myth. The asphalt is useful, but the ethereal realms of imagination and media are enhanced on the road. Pavement is part of daily life in this mobile culture. Though it is the route to the daily rut, it also is an escape from the confines of the familiar, if only for a few weekends or weeks annually, and an exercise in freedom. The road makes possible such declarations of freedom, individualism and rebellion, as the reality of life and dreams of escape merge on the highway.

Attitudes about roads are illustrated in the contrast of European and America ideas about travel. The former knew what they wanted to find and to affirm it. The latter wanted to see something new, broaden their horizons.[164] If such a broad generalization is justifiable, it must be appreciated in the context of national myths, so well encapsulated in the American West. Europeans went to the American West to see cowboys on broncos, saddle up themselves, maybe even partake of a degenerate saloon life, ala the dude ranches, which were ready to indulge their fantasies. For Americans, the road west could mean many things, including the aforementioned. But that road might also mean

---

164 Athearn, 137.

enlarging the sense of adventure and self; a route to new opportunity, whether a gold rush in the mid-19th century or a high-tech journey to ethernet and high-tech riches in more recent years. Rebellion, which could be exercised on local streets, was more fully exhibited via long roads across the country, leaving home farther away. In any case, the road did not reveal new values as much as it embellished existing ones, such as the virtues of rebellion, experiencing a frontier, finding new opportunities.

Consider, too, the somewhat cavalier attitude about roads and travel in this country, and especially in the context of the fact that motion has always been so intimate to the national DNA. Taking on the continent seemed something of a personal sport. The Canadian Highway Association, for example, needed to incentivize such a feat, and in 1911 offered a medal to the first person to cross the country via automobile. It was done 15 years later, with undoubtedly trying conditions of not just distance but mud, some "finished" roads, a challenging topography with much rock and muskeg, and few maps to speak of. Such a drive had already been done in the United States, more than two decades earlier, not waiting for roads and defined routes, let alone an association's acclaim. The trans-Canada highway did not open until in 1962 and was nearly 4,900 miles long.[165] Drivable roads across America had been in place for several decades.

In the same way that roads affirmed values, they also could be a route to imposing values on others. Until the late 19th century, there was a West or far north to be civilized, largely by bridging rivers, scaling mountains, leveling grasslands, and ultimately with paving. If one couldn't get there expeditiously, it wasn't civilized. The better the access,

---

165 Hindley, 119-120.

the more civilized it was. Conquest often meant violence, which was greatly facilitated with good roads, which were essential to enlarging the nation, geographically as well as ideologically.

As the system of roads grew, the frontier did not simply disappear. In the sense of a place untouched by civilization, it may have been physically vanquished, but the idea actually grew in the national imagination. It was an inverse relationship between roads and Frederick Jackson Turner's concept of frontier: more and better roads meant a diminution of the frontier per se. But the relationship between the roads and the idea of the frontier was a positive one. The imagined frontier grew, as more people were able to drive west or north, to experience those remnants of wild places, to witness their imagined ideas of the frontier via national parks and other out-of-the-way places. More access to symbols of a myth strengthened the myth.

The idea is illustrated masterfully in Ken Burns *The National Parks: America's Best Idea*. In part four, "Going Home," of the six-part series, it is noteworthy that in the earliest days of the parks, the first director of national parks embraced the automobile and road building. Stephen Mather believed it would increase public support for the park system. He was right. By 1920, tourism via auto outnumbered train-arrival visitation by seven to one, and the number of visitors was more than one million for the first time. It was, of course, a mixed blessing. Building a road meant an encroachment on a pristine environment. But people rushed to the great outdoors, their own sort of frontier experience. By 1925, more than two million people visited the national parks. Opposition included The Wilderness Society, founded in part to preserve nature, to lessen the emphasis on roads. But Mather persisted. More roads not only meant more access, but a more democratic approach to the parks, which would no longer be accessible only to those who could afford, in terms of both money and time, to go by train. People began "collecting" parks, and they exhibited the accomplishment with windshield stickers or a book of park-passport stamps.

The frontier had become something that belonged to everyone. That is an oxymoron, perhaps. For purists it meant a compromised wilderness or frontier, but for most Americans, the roads to and inside the parks made wilderness and frontier real and accessible, whether one chose to exercise the right or not.

The frontier

Turner found democratic individualism a product of a unique geography, one with lots of unexplored and available country, and one to be exploited by those with the physical and mental strength to do so. His multitude of definitions for frontier included the primitive, of course, but he also meant a place of opportunity, a demarcation of savagery and civilization, a line of Americanization, a route of escape from the past, or simply a harsh environment to be challenged by ranchers, miners, traders and farmers. Given such an expansive definition, Grandin called it "a state of mind."[166]

The idea of frontier expanded dramatically with roads, which took more people than ever to the places that had existed in books and movies, and allowed them to see a frontier, of sorts, at their leisure, to absorb that great American mythology more completely. The frontier was not a separate place from the road, as each became part of a whole. Later literature and film demonstrated this: the paved road became a way to exhibit the frontier spirit. The ability to redefine nature

---

166 Grandin, 115-116.

generation by generation meant the ability to resurrect oneself, a sort of cleansing, to adopt the old European myth that life in the wilds would be idyllic, in contrast to the immorality and materialism so endemic to towns and cities. The idea of fleeing to wild lands as a purification ritual was nothing new, and in fact was a centuries-old idea in Christianity, with a succession of monks and hermits going back to the Middle Ages having found freedom in uninhabited country. By 1890, civilization had prevailed, the geographic frontier having succumbed to population growth, machinery, industry and agriculture. It no longer needed conquering. But wilderness thrived, for vacationers if not conquerors.[167] Instead, the road and the auto meant an at annual rejuvenation, sort of like the tent revival, sans preachers and collection plates.

If interstates create their own climate, as noted earlier, then roads created and re-created their own environs. Wilderness was no longer untrodden and inaccessible, just farther away. Thus, pioneering was expanded to being more than an individual or a small group of individuals heading into the wilds. It became a corporate enterprise, seizing upon the ideas of individual liberty and economic opportunity.[168] Autos and roads complemented the imagined bravado and fitness that pushed one into parts unknown, places virtually unreachable only a generation or so ago.

As the idea of a frontier became more elastic, more debatable, it became something more than a border, coming, in Grandin's words, "to suggest a cultural zone or a civilizational struggle, a way of life…." Hence, the modern American could become a frontiersman by driving to a faraway place, with hiking boots, backpack and camping gear in

---

167 Roderick Frazier Nash, *Wilderness and the American Mind* (New Haven, Conn.: Yale University Press, 2001), 17-18, 48, 59, 143.

168 Grandin, 221.

the trunk. The experience could be a common one. It wasn't just a matter of wilderness making America such a contrast to the Old World, because Canada, too, had ample wilderness. But the American impulse to integrate distant places with pavement seemed much more acute than what was seen in Canada. The first cross-country drive in America was done to satisfy an urge to simply do it, and in spite of the fact that roads of the time weren't worth a damn. Horatio Jackson's 1903 journey was made for fun, and it kicked off a movement to improve nation's roads.[169]

There are myriad explanations for the contrast, such as weather, terrain and population density. But the more ephemeral idea of mindset is necessarily part of the equation. Americans wanted both the wilderness and access to it. An ocean-to-ocean road existed in the national imagination long before it existed in fact, and before autos, which merely accelerated the place of roads in the national imagination and myth. The first attempts to drive cross country via auto failed as a result of lousy or non-existent roads. Jackson was actually the third attempt. To the extent there were roads at all, they often were dirt. There was also the chronic shortage of gasoline and car parts; no maps, so the adventurers often were lost. The Jackson trip took 63 days, 12 hours, 30 minutes, from New York to San Francisco.[170] It had been 100 years since Lewis and Clark traversed the continent.

These new perceptions about venturing into the wilds may be exemplified by a cursory look some statistics for the nation's most visited national park, The Great Smoky Mountains. The vast mountain woodland has a total of 384 miles of roads in it, 238 of them paved,

---

169 Grandin, 115-116; Dayton Duncan and Ken Burns, *Horatio's Drive: America's First Road Trip* (New York: Alfred A. Knopf, 2003), 132.

170 Duncan and Burns,16-20, 116-117.

146 unpaved, as of October 2022. This for about 522,427 acres. Another very popular "wild" destination is Yellowstone National Park, with about 2,221,776 acres, and about 466 miles of roads, 310 of the miles paved. Admittedly, the questions raised may be misguided: Why go there? What does one do there? It seems to be a mode of experiencing a wild place, but it is done via pavement. A small number of visitors actually go back-country. Still, it nourishes the imagination and the myth.

Maps and GPS: An even more democratic society

Once upon a time, the frontier was remote, mysterious, even dangerous. All of that fueled the appeal, as well as the mythology, surrounding frontiers. Now, the frontier often is a distant spot on a map. Remote, yes. Mysterious, in a way, but not because we don't know what's there or that it might be untrodden ground. Dangerous, rarely, but people do idiotic things to get lost, injured, even die in the modern so-called wilderness. But remote has assumed a foremost place in the allure of frontier. And maps are a critical aid to experiencing it.

Just as roads democratized travel, maps further democratized travel by making it even more accessible. Knowledge of destinations and routes became available to anyone, even those lacking the means to travel. Travel became more economical when maps revealed the shortest, or best, route. Adventure was not lost, and may have even been enhanced with the revelation of side roads to collect significant sights on the perimeter of the primary destination. My own such experience is exemplified, among many, when one of my own young travelers pointed out that if I was going to hit the Alaska Highway via the western route, through British Columbia, then I may as well toss the fly rod in the truck and take advantage of the great streams and rivers along the way. He was right. No trek needed, just a pull-off.

Maps inform, even when they lack information, i.e., they provide a sense of density of populace and settlement, of place in the nation. One need only glimpse a road map of North America to understand that the East Coast is densely populated, compared to much of the West and North. For some, that excites the imagination: What is between those roads?

Maps can do more than just trace a route to the next town. Roads and maps helped define early America. Lewis and Clark were America's first mapping explorers. The mystery they faced was the fact that America had something, the Louisiana purchase, and now had to figure out what. Their maps and the ones by those who followed implied a sense of national purpose that was both expansionist and optimistic. When the Oregon trail was first mapped, with the second Charles Fremont expedition in 1846, it not only affirmed those national purposes, but showed settlers the way west. In the earliest days of the nation, the Missouri River was thought to provide a way to the Pacific Ocean. The Columbia River was known to run to the Pacific, and the river's latitude was about the same as the Missouri River. Therefore, it was assumed, it was only a short portage from headwaters of the Missouri to the Columbia. Central to the mission of Lewis and Clark was finding the water route across the continent. They returned to St. Louis in September 1806. A map of the expedition was published in 1814. A few decades later, in the 1840s, Fremont's expeditions provided another step into mapping the continent, including the Oregon trail.[171] Maps still define the country. What the road makes physically accessible, the map makes comprehensible.

Like horses and warships in an earlier era, roads, maps and GPS are a form of conquest. Maps and GPS help do what people have always aspired to: conquering earth, or at least the next road or town over. Even outer space is drawn into that ambition. But with maps and GPS there is now no part of earth that is totally unknown. On a more modest scale, but still in the realm of maps, the cataloguing of America's roads means it is all out there, available for one to conquer at his or her leisure. Or at least to know the possibility exists for any of us.

The right to travel, and the ability to do so, has been enhanced in recent decades with GPS, which, like interstates, is paid by government, not private enterprise, and is free for everyone. It became fully operational in 1995, with earlier versions run by the military. GPS and such devices as Google Maps have further expedited the right to motion and the impulse to do so. One can even trace progress to a destination in real time. More places, even "remote" places, are more accessible than ever. Travel may be less adventurous, but it is greatly facilitated. Therefore, the mystique of travel is redefined, because the frontier is not so much an unknown place as it is any place simply far away or someplace that one has not visited. Still, the idea of frontier is retained, perhaps even more deeply entrenched in the cultural psyche. America still values its frontier, compared to, say, a European frontier.

Finding yesterday

Roads often guide memories, and the drivers in those backward-looking vehicles invariably are disappointed to find their recollections

---

171 John Noble Wilford, *The Mapmakers* (New York: Alfred A. Knopf, 1981).

sullied by modernity or change, or even new information. Roads are the waypoints to cities large, villages small, and Eden imagined in the countryside.

Until recently, America celebrated mobility—physically and socially. The lascivious embrace of the past—such as attempts to diminish civil rights, economic opportunity and egalitarianism, or to dredge up a colonial-days understanding of the U.S. Constitution—may be unique in American history because the road, metaphorically, became a way backward, in time and myth. Instead of enlarging the ideals and myths of opportunity and egalitarianism, some recent impulses have meant valuing the sights in the rear-view mirror more than the vista from the front windshield. When the past became a model rather than a foundation, then infrastructure could more easily be left in need of better maintenance. Like an interstate system in disrepair and near collapse in some places, the American myth itself may be in need of rehabilitation and attention. Letting roads crumble, hobbling the myths, would signal a radical shift in perspective, even a contradiction to words as the base of the statue of liberty:

> *Give me your tired, your poor,*
> *Your huddled masses yearning to breathe free,*
> *The wretched refuse of your teeming shore.*
> *Send these, the homeless, tempest-tost to me,*
> *I lift my lamp beside the golden door!"*

Those words, from Emma Lazarus in 1883, are getting second thoughts from many: don't send them. Give me yesterday. Put a wall around my country and its ideals. It follows that if roads are freedom, they will become a problematic symbol for many Americans. Or will require a different kind of road in the imagination. The imagined frontier will grow even more faint if roads do not provide a way to something new and different, but a path to entrenchment.

Maybe the national symbol moved from Ellis Island to the Southwestern border, one a promise, the other a threat. Competing ideas of American mobility—and the significance of roads in facilitating that mobility—are manifest in these two structures. The first anticipates, among other things, myriad streets of endless mix, a profusion of cultures, varied people and opportunity. The web of roadways radiates outwards, both real and symbolically, to something bigger and different. The second, in contrast, means stop, no path, paved or dusty, in any direction.

Why bother?

In many respects, traveling down a new road is like reading a good mystery, i.e., where does it go? We don't want it to be a complete mystery, though some degree of uncertainty is appealing: new landscapes, stops along the way, maybe a new destination, even surviving a seedy diner with even seedier patrons. But, like the mystery solved, there is comfort in having a general idea about where it ends up, though the particulars of the route and destination can be a surprise. Risk tolerance is negotiable, such as which route to take. Some don't like high uncertainty; return to well-known places via well-known roads. Consoling. But it still is different from overly familiar home environs. The road is calculated uncertainty. Good for us timid souls who don't really want to venture for miles and days on foot across uncertain terrain. Uncertainty is interesting, to an extent; certainty is not. But the latter can be boring. One can see Denali, for example, from the paved road, and one has experienced something most never will see.

Roads are the aortas of the nation as they pump life across and into communities near and far, both geographically and demographically. Tying roads to freedom and individual rights began in the 19th century. Female activists saw a proving ground with roads—where women could do just as well as men. It only got better, as the hand-cranked starter was replaced with the electrical starter. In the 1930s, *The Green Book* was published for Black travelers, offering information on places and routes amenable to the minority populace. The vision of the publication grew along with the demands of civil rights activists a few decades later. Going down the road was a right, not something to be reserved for one part of America. Like seating in restaurants, the idea of a road and amenities excluding Black people was fading. More practically, businesses that depended on travelers realized the economic advantages to integration. Expedited roads with more travelers meant more money.

Our schizophrenia about roads is reflected in the condemnation of something that tears up the countryside and neighborhood, but then is used daily. The landscapes of modern highways are fleeting, like the landscapes of the years of life itself. A certain kind of frontier is gone, forever, but the concept remains vibrant in our mediated imaginations. And may it remain so. If the road ends, we might also.

Epilogue:

THAT OTHER ROAD

Driving is tedium and exhilaration, as anyone who has driven much—voluntarily—knows. But it is not idleness and stasis. A jaunt across America and up the Alaska Highway illustrates this well. Much to see, a long way to go. It is, for some of us, a way to stay sane in the retirement years, which expand the opportunity to act and simultaneously contract the ability to do so. Something so often overlooked is how motion, just driving down the road, keeps one sane. It is something to do, destination substituting for purpose. Ernest Hemingway's protagonist in "Big Two Hearted River" found a way to go through life without going crazy. He went fishing. A fly rod in the truck, going down the highway works wonders for the soul. The road is an elixir, social as well as individual. The pavement can be a panacea for numerous ills, small and large, as is sloshing around in a stream for a few hours after driving there.

Solitary travel is both stimulating and revolting. The challenge for the solitary traveler is to find something "out there."[172] Since one is alone, honesty is optional in terms of finding that something. Writing about one's travel is inevitably egotistical, inward looking, which itself may be a perilous sojourn. Writing is vanity, presuming that others care what one says or how it is said. The latter is the refuge of the literati—if

---

172
McMurtry, *Roads*, 23.

you've got nothing to say, do it with panache and style. But writing is a paradox, too, of both vanity and humility. This is amplified with travel writing, imposing one's perspective on faraway, unknown places. Travel also is a way for one inconsequential soul to wrap himself up in the myths of the larger culture. It may be immersion in individualism and exceptionalism, doing something unique and challenging. The rebel rebels, though the object of discontent often is undefined It is an escape, venturing into a frontier, in a historical grand tradition.

As I hit my 70th summer, maybe I'm too old. That "maybe" inevitably will become definitely. The last 4,683-mile door-to-door was 2019. So there was a precedent for this jaunt. For most of us, aging means the temptation to look backward, which is fine, for a life properly lived. But driving means the necessity of looking forward, eyes on the road ahead, using the rear-view mirror only for the occasional glimpse backward. I needed to do the journey of many thousands of miles before time sentenced me to the inertia of a back-porch rocker.

Philip Caputo, in "The Farthest Away River" in *Shadows of the Morning,* journeys to the Kongakut River, which translates from the Inuit as "farthest away." It is aptly named as it is in the far northeastern corner of the Arctic National Wildlife Refuge, and farthest away river from anywhere in the United States, going through some of the wildest parts of the continent. For Caputo, that was the attraction. Thus, the allure of driving to Alaska, my route much less wild, but still attractive for the pure sense of not just going, but going far. I'd be on pavement, mostly. But I'd be away, gratifying the motion impulse. He, too, begrudged getting old, being 55 when he made the journey with three companions from 44 to 62 years old, on a hunting trip. His endeavor in the bush was more noble, but what we had in common was an impulse to move, to go where most did not. The goal: "to flee from the familiar," among other things. His lyrical paean to motion documents the wilderness search for grizzly, caribou, sheep, and the travails of doing so, in which he revels.[173]

Motion can be a cognitive stimulant, bringing the challenge of "what next." Even a rest stop becomes significant, not only a place with restrooms and a chance to stretch, but maybe achieve a fairly safe nap. Driving can move one away from the culture's obsession with the type of car and its beauty, and toward the landscape and the path of invasion, which is the road, where even potholes matter.

Any traveler has some inkling of what is ahead, and usually anticipates it. Perhaps there is some knowledge of what is out there, real or imagined, and of what is behind us, real or imagined. The maps are paper; the roads asphalt, dirt and gravel; the movement ephemeral. At home, daily life is a checklist, cognitively or on paper, of things to do or hope to do. On the road, there is mileage, ahead and behind, a real measure of the day, affirmed with mile markers.

Something is lost when a purpose lights the highway too brightly. Destiny and purpose are life's burdens, so there is some kind of freedom with being loosed from them.

My travel raised questions: Am I looking at America, via the roads, or at myself? Valid questions of others who wrote very good road books. In summer 2019, my venture up the nicely paved Alaska Highway to Fairbanks was a retiree's lark. The goal was Fairbanks, the adventure was the drive, especially in northern Alberta, British Columbia, and Southern Yukon. I wasn't much for taking in the character of others along the way. The few I spoke with were unique, perhaps odd, I thought, to place, time and self—representing nothing

---

173 Caputo, 23, 29.

but themselves and the moment. Among the more memorable was a stop for the night at a crossroads in the Yukon, at a very modest motel. The apparent owner and full-time employee was a young woman. A brief conversation at that check-in desk included her query as to where was I from, and where was I going. I asked her the same of her. Come to find out, she had a college degree, from the University of North Carolina at Chapel Hill. I was slightly gobsmacked, and I asked why she was up here in the far corner of nowhere. Her answer was succinct, eloquent and powerful: "Because I want to be."

Here was a person unaffected by the provincialism so common in so many of the towns along the way. Clerks, waitresses, attendants who apparently were clueless when asked about the accommodations or diners in the next town over, or road conditions and distances. The lack of knowledge about where one lived was puzzling at first, in light of the extraordinary country I was experiencing. But I reminded myself, they are scratching out a living in a place they may or may not like, whether they were there by circumstances or choice, and not luxuriating in a new, faraway place. Perhaps the geographic silo in which so many resided was a matter largely subsumed by practical concerns—surviving in a remote place, in harsh environs, with those concerns overriding any impulse to indulge in highway adventures.

Such radically individualistic people represent only their own independence and individualism. But it was quite protestant of me to insist on the worth of individualism in the face of such a geography that demanded communal effort to travel, and perhaps even a lapse of one's common sense. So the loner in me, hypocritically, used a triumph of industrialism, the car, to traverse miles and imagination via that monument of social effort: tax dollars at work via machines and asphalt.

The follow up in the summer of 2023 was about several things, including an epilogue for this book. It was a panacea. For everything. Restlessness and boredom. Purposelessness. Doubts, exacerbated by age, even a few friends' complementary admonition of my "madness" to do such a thing at my age. It was familial symmetry, too, in that the trip began with one son's house, in Atlanta, journey to the other's abode, in Fairbanks, and then back to Atlanta.

One going along the Alaska Highway or the Lincoln Highway is traversing historical landmarks, with beginning and end points marked as much by time as by place. Like our imaginations, the side roads may be more interesting than the main ones. Still, they are concrete places that help one define an accomplishment for oneself or to share with others in order to spew tales of the feat.

Amplified myths: The "Alcan"

A barroom wall in Telegraph Creek, British Columbia, said it so well, recounted by Hoagland, and worthy of repeating:

> *Winding in a winding out*
> *Leaves me in serious doubt*
> *If the dude that built this road*
> *Was going to hell or coming out ....* [174]

The destination was not the so-called "last frontier." The road was the destination, with the patina of purpose—going to Fairbanks to see my oldest son. Alaska is now a land of faux frontiersmen. Or as my older son remarked several years ago about the Alaska frontier—all places are now accessible by some means. Maybe they are not trodden

---

174 Edward Hoagland, *Notes from the Century Before: A Journal from British Columbia* (New York: The Modern Library, 2002), 57.

by human feet, but they definitely are imprinted by airplanes and in the digital shadows of GPS satellites.

The Alaska Highway is largely in Canada. Its starting point appears settled, as there is a statue and marker in Dawson Creek, B.C., proclaiming the beginning of the highway. Then, it proceeds to the Yukon Territory, from near Watson Lake, going 577 miles to Port Alcan at the border with Alaska, Then, it is 200 miles to Delta Junction, the official end of the highway at mile 1,422. But the unofficial end of the highway is in Fairbanks at mile 1,523. The military highway was completed in October 1942, and opened to the public in 1948. As though some inconsequential disagreement about the end point is not enough, there can be confusion about getting there. A person is not on the Alaska Highway after crossing the border to Canada. There are three major access routes to Dawson City: from Great Falls, Montana, about 169 miles; from Ellensburg, Washington, about 596 miles; from Seattle, Washington, about 807 miles. If that is not enough, the very decisive looking outset in Dawson City, "milepost zero," is off by a few blocks, being south of the highway's actual starting point. But the marker has become reality for thousands of travelers, logged in many thousands of photos.[175]

It goes with a lot of myth, some of it properly earned, such as being the greatest military-engineering accomplishment since the Panama Canal. It was not just a matter of it being built, in 1942, in one summer, which is very short in the north country. Several other things played into the difficulty. First, mud, sometimes so deep it consumed heavy machinery, such as tractors. It was not simply leveling of ground and putting down some pavement. Second was insects, mosquitoes

---

175 *Mileposts 2021*, 50, 91, 105, 155; William Wonders , *Alaska Highway Explorer: Place Names Along the Adventure Road* (Victoria, BC: Horsdal & Schubart, 1994), 6.

and gnats that descended like a fog on workers. It was more than 1,600 miles of road across largely unexplored territory, without good maps, and without which there was no good survey of where the road would go. The muskeg at a point north of Fort Nelson even meant two miles of uninterrupted corduroying, with prodigious amounts of timber. In some places, tractors were put to work dragging trucks out of the mud, with it taking up to six hours to go 15 miles. In another place, a packhorse sunk in deep enough to die in deep mud. It sometimes is forgotten that mud and mosquitoes are major factors in a great myth.[176]

It was not just limited time to build it, terrain that varied from mountains to muskeg to numerous large rivers, and the fog of mosquitos and black flies. At first, even the name of the road was a matter of contention. The term "Alcan" highway apparently incited ire in both Canada and Alaska. A notable problem was the "pedestrian moose," which could be aggressive in mating season. The problem was frequent enough that territorial police were given butcher training and equipped with knives for the job after dispatching problematic moose. One worker on the highway found it especially notable that he did not go crazy, "as so many others did."[177]

Now, however, much of the mystique has been subsumed in travel guides. There's not a lot of mystery in what one might find along the

---

176 *National Geographic*, "Alaskan Highway an Engineering Epic," 83:2, February 1943, 143-168; University of Alaska Fairbanks archives, McDonald papers, folder 17, "The Alaska Highway: The Muskeg Mystery," by John M. Holzworth; McDonald papers, The Seattle Times, "Their Traffic Problems Include Moose," Fairbanks papers, box 1, folder 1.

177 University of Alaska archives, McDonald papers, folder 17, "The Alaska Highway: The Muskeg Mystery," by John M. Holzworth; "Farewell to Jangling 'Alcan,'" Fairbanks papers, box 1, folder 1, July 2, 1943, no newspaper name given; "The Country Speaks: Alaska: 'Alcan' Taken Over the Bumps," by Fergus Hoffman, no newspaper name, date given; Ray C. Haman papers, Haman diary, Oct. 1943.

highway. There are ample bears, buffalo, mountain goats, moose and deer, especially in northern British Columbia and the Yukon Territory. The highway and the different access routes to it are well documented. In *Mileposts*, one can find several hundred pages of detailed maps and descriptions of sightseeing opportunities, as well as restaurants and hotels. *Bell's Alaska Highway* provides information to the tenth of mile/kilometer on what to expect. In addition to the usual eateries and stopovers, one could read, for example, that at km 641 there is parking at the south end of the Racing River bridge, where there's fishing for arctic grayling and Dolly Varden trout. Go a little farther, to km 1063.1 on the lower Rancheria River and get the fly rod out. Use small black flies. In the Yukon, at km 1419.4, one is near an airport and downtown Whitehorse. At Hi Country RV Park, the amenities include cable TV, a laundromat, showers, and an RV wash.[178]

Still, it is a storied highway, and the subject of numerous books. That highway does on an epic scale what roads in the lower 48 have done on a lesser scale. Beyond its original rationalization, the Alaska highway now is testament to the important idea of the enduring frontier. The state calls itself the last frontier, and those of us who take on the challenge of driving what is actually a Canadian highway, can presume an aura of frontiersmanship.

It has been romanticized from the beginning. Such a view is illustrated well in Jim Christy's *Rough Road to the North: Travels Along the Alaska Highway*. It is his personal story, admiring almost everyone he meets—in bars, restaurants, driving, and so on. He is taken by Turner's frontier myth, finding genuine heroism in the construction of the highway, from clerks and cowpunchers with feet on the ground,

---

178 Bells Travel Guides: Alaska Highway Travel Log, bellsalaska.com, accessed May 2023.

mixing grueling work with boredom and harsh weather. He commends
people in such places as the Yukon Territory. The jobs are pedestrian,
whether prospecting, logging or clerking. Life is "pale and cold."
But the people are commended, remnant frontiersmen who merit
recognition on the pages of literary geniuses such as Jack London.[179]

Another volume's recognition is even more explicitly admiring,
and is titled *Romance of the Alaska Highway*, by Philip Godsell. It was
written in 1944, when the accomplishment of building the road was
fresher in the minds of people, along with Pearl Harbor and fears
of invasion via Alaska. The remoteness is reflected in Alaska's sparse
population in 1940, just over 72,500 people. The initiative to build
a road connecting Alaska to the lower 48 began in 1928, sporting a
slogan, "Seven Million Dollars Purchased Alaska for the States, Seven
Million More Will Make Alaska One of the United States."[180]

The *National Geographic* article noted above, from 1943, gave a
relatively hard-nosed, realistic view of the highway. A few decades later,
the magazine titles an article on the same subject "Alaska Highway:
Wilderness Escape Route," and provided a more romantic perspective
of the road, putting it in a very different, peacetime-leisure context. The
builders' first winter there, it dropped to as low as minus 71 degrees
Fahrenheit. A resident in Contact Creek, Yukon, remembered rescuing
21 people whose cars had quit. They crowded into a diner, where the
generator also quit because the diesel fuel gelled. The author of the
article found it all rather incredible, and figured many of the individuals

---

179 Jim Christy, *Rough Road to the North: Travels along the Alaska Highway* (Garden City,
     N.Y.: Doubleday & Co., 1980), 151.

180 Philip Godsell, *The Romance of the Alaska Highway* (Toronto: The Ryerson Press,
     1944), 122.

were running to or from something. It's lonely, the climate brutal, the people and community spirit admirable.[181]

There were the adventurers of the late 1940s and early 1950s who drove to Alaska for various reasons, some to look for jobs and fantasies of riches in the new promised land, a sort of new gold rush. There were military men being transferred to bases. Others were homesteaders, sightseers, and some just for the hell of it. Such as the three University of Oklahoma students who believed they had made record time in getting 2,162 miles from Fairbanks to Edmonton, Alberta. There were outdoorsmen, too, looking for the hunting and fishing riches of the north country. Edmonton residents and others who lived along the highway cashed in on the travel. The constant in the equation was the impulse to move. Driving a road for no particular reason was nothing new in the national story.[182]

In November 1942, an opening ceremony was held for the pioneer highway. That event was not, obviously, marking the completion of the highway. The ceremony at Soldiers Summit, Yukon, included the usual speeches by various dignitaries. But among the remarks were a few that reflected some remorse for the end of real pioneering, the last wilderness having been conquered, in a way.[183]

What we think is there is much more important than what merely exists there. It's not just pavement. Our imaginations affirm an idea, rising to the status of myth in our national psyche. Like the "Wild West," it is physically there, but not as written in our collective

---

181 *National Geographic*, "Alaska Highway: Wilderness Escape Route," by Richard Olsenius, Nov. 1991, 68-99, 81.

182 David A. Remley, *Crooked Road: The Story of the Alaska Highway* (New York: McGraw Hill Books, 1976), 187-188.

183 Remley, 88-89.

imaginations. It can illustrate, or exaggerate, the individualism impulse, the claim to uniqueness, rebellion, or just a path to a frontier, imagined or real. The Alaska Highway is remote, but that remoteness is pretense of the frontier. Perhaps, as Hoagland, notes, it was frontier because nobody had the desire the settle down there:

> The delights of the Alaska Highway are for somebody else to explain. They involve the mathematics of distance and something about the gray gravel against the jackpine. The tourists stream by with the headlights on because of the dust, fearfully tired. …. If this is a frontier, as they seem to believe, it's because, unlike Wriglesorths' Chutine [an abandoned settlement in British Columbia], for instance, nobody has had the desire to settle down here. It's like standing at the World's Fair and watching a squadron of people file by, registering exactly the same expression. They get out of their cars every minute or so and think, The Yukon! ….[184]

A summer jaunt, 2023

It's not my last chance to do stupid things, but it may well be my last chance to do this particular one --10,000 miles in a summer. So, I headed from the urban wilderness and into the American West, and into Canadian wilds with my McNally's and MapQuest, even *Mileposts,* the latter for the especially allegedly wild and risky Alaska Highway. McNally's and MapQuest are Old Testaments and New Testaments for the highway traveler. *Mileposts* is an even newer testament for a very recent road. Having driven the Alaska Highway, a few reactions to any mention of such a trek evoked a response, perhaps admiration, even envy and a complementary admonition. However,

---

184   Hoagland 88-89.

braving a few miles through downtown Atlanta is far riskier than the few hundred solitary miles on the plains of Alberta.

Shortly out of Atlanta, one of the first things to come up on the radio was the Eagles, "Hotel California," with the refrain "Some dance to remember, some dance to forget." So it goes with driving. The number of people on these interstates reminds me that my quest is nothing unique or special, especially when I note the camper-vehicles. It is part of a culture of motion, an impulse that amplifies values and myths, and does not create them. It is a sub-culture of generally co-operative strangers. What they have in common is not a place of origin or destination, but simply "going." The highway is where entertainment and obligation simultaneously reside, helping one make a living and escaping it. A long drive is its own purpose. Security is a full tank of gasoline, and comfort is a wide, graveled spot in the road for a nap (they call them rest areas in Canada), and peanut butter crackers in the food sack.

Driving and thinking are complementary. It at least demands consideration of where to have supper, or where to spend the night. The Rand-McNally's supersedes GPS on this count. The former provides a picture of where the next significant crossroads might be. That does not always work, though, as I found in the Yukon and British Columbia, where that next crossroad might offer nothing, not even a gasoline station. I had a five-gallon gasoline can for insurance.

Sights are collected, sort of like accumulating refrigerator magnets. It was a low-level gratification in that only I was there to appreciate the scenery. Still, I collected. Motion is relaxation, necessarily, because one simply cannot be in a state of tension for a long drive. I found my drive on the Alaska Highway, as well as to and from that particular section of the journey, an exemplary curative for lacking purpose. Driving to Alaska is not defensible, in practical or economic terms. Flying is quicker and cheaper if destination is the sole purpose. However, with flying something is lost, such as the beauty of the oddly named Toad River. Or experiencing the traveling perfection of Fast Eddy's in Tok, Alaska, had I soared over that place with unparalleled omelets, good beds, reasonable prices, and a travelers' crowd of denim, unkempt hair, scruffy sneakers and boots.

Part of the charm with time on the road is learning to appreciate things that might otherwise go unnoticed. In my case, it was place names. Some are blandly predictable, for a person who got there first to found a settlement or opened a trading post, or a creek getting the moniker of an early explore, trapper or miner. Others are less obvious, or need some translation from Indian names. A couple are downright puzzling, such as British Columbia's "70-mile House" and "150-Mile House" and a few others with a "mile house" moniker. Miles from what? Turns out to be the distance from mile zero on the Old Cariboo Road, not much known now. And why miles in a place that measures distance in kilometers? "Yukon," predictably, is from an Indian name for "big river," the biggest one in the Canadian northwest and interior Alaska. The outset of the highway in Dawson Creek is for a geologist who was part of an 1873-75 survey of the region. The town boomed with arrival of troops in WWII to begin the highway. The aptly named Summit Lake is near the highest point on the Alaska Highway, at 4,250 feet. Thankfully, William Wonders, of the University of Alberta, published a book in 1994 on place names.

Toad River may strike some, as it did me, an odd name for such a beautiful river in such a scenic area. It is a sizeable river of clear water, rapids, and lined with boulders scoured near white, scenically scattered with washed-down timbers. But perhaps the person who named it, an early Hudson Bay Company explorer, was a little less taken with scenery and more struck by the huge toads he found in large numbers along the banks of the river, some up to one-and-one-half pounds. Local Indians told him there were bigger ones around.

In the Yukon Territory, Whitehorse is named not for equines but for the label attached to rapids, which vanished with the construction of a hydroelectric dam in 1959. Early explorers thought the rapids looked like the manes of white horses. One can't help but wonder what happened for "Destruction Bay" to get its name. It's a fairly recent settlement, built in 1942 by the Army Corp of Engineers and earning its name with high-wind destruction of buildings and materials not long after it was built.

When one gets to Alaska, there is Tok, an Indian name for a nearby river. Some confusion apparently arose over this one because some thought it a WWII name-abbbreviation for "Camp Tokyo." North Pole, near Fairbanks, reflects aspirations of another WW II community. They hoped to attract a toy manufacturer. Fairbanks' name is more bland, for an early 20th-century Indiana senator who was the friend of a local judge. Some names are more educational than others, a particular example being "Squanga Lake," which is obviously Indian, but named for pygmy whitefish that live in only a few lakes in Southern Yukon.[185] With the miles, gross generalizations accrue about other travelers, attendants at various restaurants or motels or gasoline stations, and even concerning the towns along the way. Too often, motels, eateries, and gas stations are not where I think they should be. A late-night drive through Watson Lake, Yukon, created some trepidation when no self-serve fuel stops were self-serving. No motel lobbies

---

185 Place-name information is from Wonders, *Alaska Highway Explorer*.

were open. Daytime naps at gravel pull offs in the Yukon and British
Columbia became routine. In Saskatchewan, a route recommended
by my older son, an outdoorsman with better sense of direction and a
fondness for alleged shortcuts, turned into a midnight nightmare. The
backroads went through towns without a light on, let alone any service
stops.

Sit-down meals, usually one per day, in the evening, could be a
comfortable respite or a greasy wide spot that enhanced appreciation
for getting back on the road. This aspect of travel really depended on
how important food was for a person, when to take a break, and the
suitability of crackers and apples for lunch, not to forget gas-station
pastry and coffee for breakfast.

One learns that the beauty of a landscape is a relative thing. An
"ugly" South Dakota was bemoaned by one travel writer as being too
brown and dusty, for lacking greenery and being so unlike his native
region in the East. Maybe his eyes were closed on that part of his cross-
country trip. Sameness is not beauty. In fact, contrast can be striking,
such as the Western Route to the Alaska Highway, with its mountains
and rivers, versus the Eastern Route's unending sea of greenery in the
Alberta plains. It seems we ought to travel in order to appreciate the
variety, not condemn it.

A drive being long, even tiring, is not a bad thing. The Eagles
came on the radio as I crossed the American plains states. In "Take it
easy," I was reminded, "don't let the sound of your own wheels drive
you crazy." Good advice on I-90, Wyoming, Idaho, Washington,
for 853 miles that day, July 1. It helped induce a near-meditative
relaxation, letting go.

A road is not always paved, let alone adorned with lane
designations and edge stripes. A transition from pavement to gravel to

pavement was common. If one wanted sameness, go home. The route in Northern British Columbia and in the Yukon was the best part of drive perhaps, and terrible driving. A lot of road work meant miles of gravel, potholes, long delays, much dust. And there was the haze from the thousands of acres burning far enough away to not close the road, but near enough to necessitate rolling up the windows and using the vehicle's air conditioning. The smoke recalled the contradiction of travel itself, an unnatural act of immersing oneself in nature. The smoke is a result of a natural phenomenon—wildfire. But the fires are exacerbated by something quite unnatural and immediate, the human-caused warming and extreme weather. Still, the landscape was beautiful, the wildlife so abundant one had to be alert for the sake of safety.

A journey anywhere is always more exciting than the trip home. The former is anticipation and excitement. The latter is grim determination. And so it is with this book. The destination already has been determined. The obstacles are in the footnotes, easily skirted, and the discovery—I vainly hope—is in moving through the pages. 10,396 miles. Now, back home, the comfort of the familiar, and the discomfort of sameness. Already, there are thoughts of the asphalt balm.

American Beauty, '57 Plymouth Fury

The 1957 Plymouth Fury was among the most fashionable of the era's autos, as well as being beautifully powerful. The manufacturer's suggested retail price was about $2,900, with only a little over 7,400 of them built in 1957. The aesthetics of this model, as well as others of the period, are worthy of note not only because of their looks, but also because they were something of an accent to the great industrial triumph of road building, which continues to this day. The pavement was an accent to the auto, like a frame accentuates the art within. (Painting by Jim Stovall)

ACKNOWLEDGMENTS

Jim Stovall, for several things: artwork, advice on self-publishing, for reading and editing, and for not commenting on my lack of acuity about the digital world. To both Jim and Sally Stovall for reminding me of the absolute madness of driving to Fairbanks, at my age, and with western Canada afire. The admonition was inspirational, so I went.

Paul Ashdown, for encouragement when my enthusiasm waned. And critical comments about my use of the term "myth."

Robert and Trang, for giving me a reason to get the hell out of the house and for providing a sympathetic ear. And they provided a takeoff and endpoint for my 10,000-mile summer.

Danny and Gretchen, especially for giving me an excuse to drive to Alaska, yet again.

To the reference desk at the Blount County Public Library, especially Brennan LeQuire, who found arcane material and did not ask pointed questions, such as "what the hell are you looking at that for?"

To the folks at the University of Alaska Fairbanks archives, for facilitating the search in their Alaska Highway files, especially Fawn Carter, assistant archivist, Alaska and Polar Regions Collection & Archives.

Donn King at Hidden Mentor Media for his help in the design of the cover and interior of this book as well as figuring out the maddening process of publication.

BIBLIOGRAPHY

Arsenault, Raymond, *Freedom Riders: 1961 and the Struggle for Racial Justice* (New York: Oxford University Press, 2006).

Ashdown, Paul and Edward Caudill, *Imagining Wild Bill: James Butler Hickok in War, Media and Memory* (Carbondale, Illinois: Southern Illinois University Press, 2020).

Athearn, Robert G., *The Mythic West in Twentieth Century America* (Lawrence, Kansas: The University Press of Kansas, 1986).

Brands, H.W., *Dreams of El Dorado: A History of the American West* (New York: Basic Books, 2019).

Bruder, Jessica, *Nomadland: Surviving America in the Twenty-first Century* (New York: W.W. Norton, 2017).

Caputo, Philip, *The Longest Road: Overland in Search of America, from Key West to the Arctic Ocean* (New York: Henry Holt and Company, 2013).

Child, Lee, *A Jack Reacher Novel: Nothing to Lose* (New York: Del, 2014); *Blue Moon* (New York: Random House, 2019).

Christy, Jim, *Rough Road to the North: Travels Along the Alaska Highway* (Toronto: Doubleday, 1980).

Coates, Kenneth S., and William R. Morrison, *The Alaska Highway in World War II: The U.S. Army of Occupation in Canada's Northwest* (Oklahoma City: University of Oklahoma Press, 2015).

Conover, Ted, *The Routes of Man: The Roads are Changing the World We Live in and the Way We Live Today* (New York: Alfred A. Knopf, 2010).

Davies, Pete, *American Road: The Story of an Epic Transcontinental Journey at the Dawn of the Motor Age* (New York: Henry Holt and Company, 2002).

Dellinger, Matt, *Interstate 69: The Unfinished History of the Last Great American Highway* (New York: Scribner 2010).

Dollarhide, William, *Map Guide to American Migration Routes, 1735-1815* (Bountiful, Utah: HeritageQuest, 2000).

Duncan, Dayton and Ken Burns, *Horatio's Drive: America's First Road Trip* (New York: Alfred A. Knopf, 2003).

Eisenhower, Dwight D., *At Ease: Stories I Tell to Friends* (Garden City, New York: Doubleday, 1967).

Gael, Hoal, *The Lincoln Highway: The Story of a Crusade That Made Transportation History* (New York: Dodd, Mead & Co., 1935).

Gordon, John Steele, "Engine of Liberation," *American Heritage*, November 1996, pp. 42-76.

Grandin, Greg, *The End of the Myth: From the Frontier to the Border Wall in the Mind of America* (New York: Metropolitan Books, 2019).

Harrison, Fraser, *Infinite West: Travels in South Dakota* (Pierre, SD: South Dakota State Historical Society Press, 2012).

Heike, Paul, *The Myths that Made America: An Introduction to American Studies* (New Rockford, ND: Transcript Verlag, 2014).

Hindley, Geoffrey, *A History of Roads* (Secaucus, NJ: The Citadel Press, 1972).

Hokanson, Drake, *The Lincoln Highway: Main Street Across America* (Iowa City: University of Iowa Press, 1988).

Laderman, David, *Driving Vision: Exploring the Road Movie* (Austin: University of Texas Press, 2002).

Jaffe, Eric, *The Kings Best Highway: The Lost History of the Boston Post Road, The Route that Made America* (New York: Scribner, 2010).

Levy, Bernard-Henri, *American Vertigo: Traveling America in the Footsteps of Tocqueville* (New York: Random House, 2006).

Lewis, Tom, *Divided Highways: Building the Interstate Highway, Transforming American Life* (New York: Viking Penguin, 1997).

The Lincoln Highway Association, *The Lincoln Highway: The Story of a Crusade that Made Transportation History* (New York: Dodd Mean & Co., 1935).

Lipset, Seymour Martin, *Continental Divide* (Oxfordshire, England: Routledge Press, 1990).

Lule, Jack, *Daily News, Eternal Stories: The Mythological Role of Journalism* (New York: The Guilford Press, 2001).

Malone, Michael P. and Richard W. Etulain, *The American West: A Twentieth-Century History* (Lincoln: University of Nebraska Press, 1989).

McCarthy, Cormac, *The Road* (New York: Vintage International, 2006).

McGrath, Roger, *Gunfighters, Highwaymen and Vigilantes: Violence in the Frontier* (Berkeley: University of California Press, 1984).

McMurtry, Larry, *Roads: Driving America's Great Highways* (New York: Simon and Schuster, 2000).

McPhee, John, *Coming into the Country* (New York: Farrar, Straus and Giroux, 1977).

The Milepost: Alaska Travel Planner 2021 (Anchorage, AK: MCC Magazines, 2021).

Mills, Katie, *The Road Story and the Rebel: Moving Through Film, Fiction and Television* (Carbondale: Southern Illinois University Press, 2006).

Moon, William Least Heat, *Blue Highways* (Robbinsdale, Minn.: Fawcett Crest, 1982).

Murdoch, David Hamilton, *The American West: The Invention of a Myth* (Las Vegas: University of Nevada Press, 2001).

Nash, Roderick Frazier, *Wilderness and the American Mind*, fourth edition (New Haven, Conn.: Yale University Press, 2001).

Preston, Howard Lawrence, *Dirt Roads to Dixie: Accessibility and Modernization in the South, 1885-1935* (Knoxville: University of Tennessee Press, 1991),

Primeau, Ronald, editor, *American Road Literature* (Ipswich, Mass.: Salem Press, 2013).

Reid, Mayne, *The Boy Hunters* (New York: Lasso Press, 2015 reprint of 1852 edition).

Remley, David A., *Crooked Road: The Story of the Alaska Highway* (New York: McGraw-Hill Book Co., 1976).

Robinson, James Oliver, *American Myth, American Reality* (New York: Hill and Wang, 1980).

Rose, Albert C. and Carl Rokeman, *Historic American Roads: From Frontier Trails to Superhighways* (New York: Crown Publishers, 1976).

Ryan, Alan, editor, *The Readers Companion to Alaska* (New York: Harcourt Brace, Inc., 1997).

Smith, Henry Nash, *Virgin Land: The American West as Symbol and Myth* (Cambridge, Mass.: Harvard University Press, 1950),

Sorin, Gretchen, *Driving While Black: African American Travel and the Road to Civil Rights* (New York: Liveright Publishers, 2020).

Stager, Claudette and Martha Carver, *Looking Beyond the Highway: Dixie Roads and Culture* (Knoxville: University of Tennessee Press, 2006).

Stegner, Wallace, *Where the Bluebird Sings to the Lemonade Springs: Living and Writing in the West* (New York: Penguin Books, 1992).

Steinbeck, John, *Travels with Charley* (New York: Viking Press, 1962).

Swift, Earl, *The Big Roads: The Untold Story of the Engineers, Visionaries, and Trailblazers Who Created the American Superhighways* (New York: Mariner Books, 2011).

Swift, Earl, *Divided Highways: Building the Interstate Highways, Transforming American Life* (New York: Viking, Penguin, 1997).

Twichell, Heath, *Northwest Epic: The Building of the Alaska Highway* (New York: St. Martin's Press, 1992).

Williams, Mark, *Road Movies: The Complete Guide to Cinema on Wheels* (New York: Proteus, 1982).

Newspapers and magazines

Agee, James, "The Great American Roadside," *Fortune*, July-Sept. 1934, v. 10, pp. 53-63, 172, 174, 177.

Atlantic Monthly, "Travel in the United States," April 1867.

Brinkley, Douglas, "The Most American of the American Literary Genres is Nearly as Old as the Motorcar Itself," *American Heritage* 47:7, November 1996.

DiLorenzo, Thomas J., "The Culture of Violence in the American West," *Independent Review*, Fall 2020.

Gordon, John Steele, "Engine of Liberation," *American Heritage*, Nov. 1996, 42-76.

MacKaye, Benton and Lewis Mumford, "Townless Highways for the Motorist," *Harpers Magazine,* August 1931, 347-356.

McCarty, Joe, "The Lincoln Highway," *American Heritage*, June 1974, v. 25, no. 4, pp. 32-39, 89.

New York Review of Books, "Sacagewea's Nickname: Essays on the American West," 2001: 7.

Time Magazine, "Ode to the Road," Sept. 10, 1965.

Film

"Bonnie and Clyde" (1967)

"Easy Rider" (1969).

"Jack Reacher" (2012).

"Nomadland" (2020).

"Thelma and Louise" (1991)

Other books by Edward Caudill

Sherman's March in Myth and Memory (The American Crisis Series: Books on the Civil War Era) with Paul Ashdown

The Myth of Nathan Bedford Forrest (The American Crisis Series: Books on the Civil War Era) with Paul Ashdown

The Mosby Myth: A Confederate Hero in Life and Legend (The American Crisis Series: Books on the Civil War Era) with Paul Ashdown

Inventing Custer: The Making of an American Legend (The American Crisis Series: Books on the Civil War Era) with Paul Ashdown

Intelligently Designed: How Creationists Built the Campaign Against Evolution

Imagining Wild Bill: James Butler Hickok in War, Media, and Memory (Engaging the Civil War) with Paul Ashdown

Murder Most Criminous: The Cases of William Roughead, Father of Modern True Crime Literature, with Jim Stovall

Vietnam Voices: Stories of Tennesseans Who Served in Vietnam, 1965-1975 (co-editor with Jim Stovall and William Minser) (volumes 1-4)

INDEX

www.ingramcontent.com/pod-product-compliance
Lightning Source LLC
Chambersburg PA
CBHW070706130626
46553CB00005B/1866

Praise for Christina McKnight's Novels

THE THIEF STEALS HER EARL

"When I started reading this book I could not put it down...it caused another book-hangover for me. I wanted to see how things would go when the truth of Judith came out and how Simon was going to handle it...loved it."-*Sissy's Book Review*

"Jude and Cart's story is such a delight! So refreshing to see the hero shy, socially awkward and not super wealthy. I love it...This was definitely one of the best books I've read this summer." -*Reviews from a Thrifty Mom*

FORGOTTEN NO MORE

"This author has made me love historical romance again." -*TwinsieTalk Book Reviews*

HIDDEN NO MORE

"The storyline was really good, the writing was great. So smooth and engaging, I was able to zip right through the story, it flowed so well. I love finding new to me authors and with this wonderfully written story by Ms. McKnight I've found a new historical romance author."-*Bound by Books*

CHRISTMAS EVER MORE

"*Christmas Ever More* was a wonderfully written festive novella full of hope, renewal, love, and new beginnings. If you're a fan of Christina's Lady Forsaken series, this is a must. Even if you aren't caught up, this stands well enough on its own to be a lovely addition to your holiday reading list."-*Literal Addiction*

BOOKS BY CHRISTINA MCKNIGHT

FORTUNE'S FINAL FOLLY

FORTUNES OF FATE SERIES

Christina McKnight

ISBN-13: 978-1-945089-53-4
ISBN-10: 1-945089-53-9

La Loma Elite Publishing

Christina@christinamcknight.com